American Sh

Selected and edited by
Chris Brown

With activities by
Janet and Andrew Goodwyn

Oxford University Press

Oxford University Press, Walton Street, Oxford OX2 6DP

Oxford New York Toronto
Delhi Bombay Calcutta Madras Karachi
Petaling Jaya Singapore Hong Kong Tokyo
Nairobi Dar es Salaam Cape Town
Melbourne Auckland

and associated companies in
Berlin Ibadan

Oxford is a trade mark of Oxford University Press

© Selection: Chris Brown 1992

© Activities: Andrew and Janet Goodwyn 1992

ISBN 0 19 831282 2

Set by Pentacor PLC, High Wycombe, Bucks

Printed in Great Britain at the University Press, Cambridge.

The cover painting is reproduced by permission of the National
Museum of American Art, Washington D. C./Art Resource, N. Y.
1986.6.92 Edward Hopper. Cape Cod Morning. 1950

Also available in the *Oxford Literature Resources* series:

Contemporary Stories 1	0 19 831251 2
Contemporary Stories 2	0 19 831254 7
Stories from South Asia	0 19 831255 5
Science Fiction Stories	0 19 831261 X
Fantasy Stories	0 19 831262 8
Sport	0 19 831264 4
Autobiography	0 19 831265 2
Crime Stories	0 19 831280 6
Scottish Short Stories	0 19 831281 4

Contents

Acknowledgements

The editor and publisher are grateful for permission to include the following copyright stories in this collection.

Truman Capote, 'Miriam' from *The Selected Writings of Truman Capote*, © 1945; © renewed 1973 by Conde Nast Publications, Inc. Reprinted by permission of Random House, Inc. Originally appeared in *Madamoiselle*. **William Faulkner**, 'Dry September' from *These Thirteen* in *The Collected Short Stories of William Faulkner Volume II*, copyright William Faulkner. Reprinted by permission of Curtis Brown Ltd, London. **Langston Hughes**, 'Thank You, M'am' from *Sudden Fiction* (Penguin). Reprinted by permission of David Higham Associates Ltd. **Valerie Miner**, 'Misty, Tiled Chambers' from *Trespassing and Other Stories* (Methuen). Reprinted by permission of Artellus Limited. **Zora Neale Hurston**, 'Sweat' from *I Love Myself When I Am Laughing*. A Zora Neale Hurston Reader, ed. Alice Walker © 1979 by Alice Walker. Reprinted by permission of Harper Collins Publishers. **Sylvia Plath**, 'Superman and Paula Brown's New Snowsuit' from *Johnny Panic and the Bible of Dreams*. Reprinted by permission of Faber & Faber Ltd. **Philip Roth**, 'The Conversion of the Jews' from *Goodbye Columbus*. Reprinted by permission of Andre Deutsch Ltd. **William Saroyan**, 'The Idea in the Back of my Brother's Head' from *The Whole Voyald and Other Stories*. Reprinted by permission of Laurence Pollinger Ltd on behalf of William Saroyan Foundation. **John Steinbeck**, 'Breakfast' from *The Long Valley*, © 1938 by John Steinbeck. Reprinted by permission of Curtis Brown Ltd, London. **James Thurber**, 'The Catbird Seat' from *The Thurber Carnival* written and illustrated by James Thurber (Hamish Hamilton, 1945) © 1945 by James Thurber. Reprinted by permission of the publisher. **John Updike**, 'The Happiest I've Been' from *Forty Stories*. Reprinted by permission of Andre Deutsch Ltd.

Every effort has been made to secure all permissions prior to publication. If contacted, the publisher will be pleased to rectify any errors or omissions at the earliest opportunity.

Preface

The American poet, Randall Jarrell, once wrote that selecting short stories for a collection was like trying to put a zoo in a wardrobe – by the time you have managed to push the giraffe in there is little room for anything else. Choosing stories for this selection proved difficult simply because there was so much good material to choose from. If this particular 'zoo in a wardrobe' encourages readers to begin exploring the richness and diversity of American fiction, it will have served one of its main purposes.

American literature – especially the short story – for which American writers seem to have a particular flair – reflects the richness and diversity of America itself. Geographically the country stretches from the Arctic wastes of Alaska to the deserts of New Mexico; from the teeming streets of New York through the rich farmlands of the Mid-West and the 'cowboy' country of Colorado and Nevada to the Pacific Ocean. And many of these landscapes are depicted in the stories that have been chosen.

The question of America's social, cultural and racial complexity is also central to its literature and certainly to this selection. For several centuries America has provided a new beginning for successive waves of immigrants from every corner of the world – Ireland, China, Greece, Italy, Russia, Poland, Malaya, Scandinavia... (Black Americans, it is important to remember, came to America as slaves not as immigrants; Faulkner's story, *Dry September*, is a grim reminder of this.) Roth's story is set amongst a community of Jewish immigrants, Plath's father was of German stock, Saroyan depicts the Armenian community he grew up in, Hughes and Hurston derive their fiction from the black experience of American life. The themes raised by such cultural diversity are of course also relevant to today's multi-racial Britain.

This selection may also lead to a consideration of 'British culture' and how the influence of American culture on this (in its widest sense) is inescapable. Think of the many soap operas, films, news items, advertisements, products, etc. that are either American or based on American ideas. Some have argued that this pervasive influence popularizes superficial values, such as materialism, sentimentality, 'macho' toughness, and moral simplicities: the world according to *Dallas, The Waltons*, Coca-Cola advertisements, Disneyland and Rambo. In this selection the reader should, it is hoped, find a sampling of American culture at its best – with more realistic experiences of everyday life in America. Readers will no doubt see the contrasts between these two worlds – crudely between 'Hollywood' and 'life' – and this may lead to some interesting work.

In the Activities section there are background notes on the authors included in the selection, ideas for follow-on work, and suggestions for further reading. The contrasts between American English and Standard English are introduced, and more generally the activities provide a whole range of spoken and written outcomes in line with the National Curriculum at Key Stage 4 and Scottish requirements for Standard Grade.

Chris Brown

Miriam

Truman Capote

For several years, Mrs H. T. Miller had lived alone in a pleasant apartment (two rooms with kitchenette) in a remodeled brownstone near the East River. She was a widow: Mr H. T. Miller had left a reasonable amount of insurance. Her interests were narrow, she had no friends to speak of, and she rarely journeyed farther than the corner grocery. The other people in the house never seemed to notice her: her clothes were matter-of-fact, her hair iron-gray, clipped and casually waved; she did not use cosmetics, her features were plain and inconspicuous, and on her last birthday she was sixty-one. Her activities were seldom spontaneous: she kept the two rooms immaculate, smoked an occasional cigarette, prepared her own meals and tended a canary.

Then she met Miriam. It was snowing that night. Mrs Miller had finished drying the supper dishes and was thumbing through an afternoon paper when she saw an advertisement of a picture playing at a neighborhood theater. The title sounded good, so she struggled into her beaver coat, laced her galoshes and left the apartment, leaving one light burning in the foyer: she found nothing more disturbing than a sensation of darkness.

The snow was fine, falling gently, not yet making an impression on the pavement. The wind from the river cut only at street crossings. Mrs Miller hurried, her head bowed, oblivious as a mole burrowing a blind path. She stopped at a drugstore and bought a packet of peppermints.

A long line stretched in front of the box office; she took her place at the end. There would be (a tired voice groaned) a short wait for all seats. Mrs Miller rummaged in her leather handbag till she collected exactly the correct change for admission. The line seemed to be taking its own time and, looking around for some distraction, she suddenly became conscious of a little girl standing under the edge of the marquee.

Her hair was the longest and strangest Mrs Miller had ever seen: absolutely silver-white, like an albino's. It flowed waist-length in smooth, loose lines. She was thin and fragilely constructed. There was a simple, special elegance in the way she stood with her thumbs in the pockets of a tailored plum-velvet coat.

Mrs Miller felt oddly excited, and when the little girl glanced toward her, she smiled warmly. The little girl walked over and said, 'Would you care to do me a favor?'

'I'd be glad to, if I can,' said Mrs Miller.

'Oh, it's quite easy. I merely want you to buy a ticket for me; they won't let me in otherwise. Here, I have the money.' And gracefully she handed Mrs Miller two dimes and a nickel.

They went into the theater together. An usherette directed them to a lounge; in twenty minutes the picture would be over.

'I feel just like a genuine criminal,' said Mrs Miller gaily, as she sat down. 'I mean that sort of thing's against the law, isn't it? I do hope I haven't done the wrong thing. Your mother knows where you are, dear? I mean she does, doesn't she?'

The little girl said nothing. She unbuttoned her coat and folded it across her lap. Her dress underneath was prim and dark blue. A gold chain dangled about her neck, and her fingers, sensitive and musical-looking, toyed with it. Examining her more attentively, Mrs Miller decided the truly distinctive feature was not her hair, but her eyes; they were hazel, steady, lacking any childlike quality whatsoever and, because of their size, seemed to consume her small face.

Mrs Miller offered a peppermint. 'What's your name, dear?'

'Miriam,' she said, as though, in some curious way, it were information already familiar.

'Why, isn't that funny – my name's Miriam, too. And it's not a terribly common name either. Now, don't tell me your last name's Miller!'

'Just Miriam.'

'But isn't that funny?'

'Moderately,' said Miriam, and rolled the peppermint on her tongue.

Mrs Miller flushed and shifted uncomfortably. 'You have such a large vocabulary for such a little girl.'

'Do I?'

'Well, yes,' said Mrs Miller, hastily changing the topic to: 'Do you like the movies?'

'I really wouldn't know,' said Miriam. 'I've never been before.'

Women began filling the lounge; the rumble of the newsreel bombs exploded in the distance. Mrs Miller rose, tucking her purse under her arm. 'I guess I'd better be running now if I want to get a seat,' she said. 'It was nice to have met you.'

Miriam nodded ever so slightly.

It snowed all week. Wheels and footsteps moved soundlessly on the street, as if the business of living continued secretly behind a pale but impenetrable curtain. In the falling quiet there was no sky or earth, only snow lifting in the wind, frosting the window glass, chilling the rooms, deadening and hushing the city. At all hours it was necessary to keep a lamp lighted, and Mrs Miller lost track of the days: Friday was no different from Saturday and on Sunday she went to the grocery: closed, of course.

That evening she scrambled eggs and fixed a bowl of tomato soup. Then, after putting on a flannel robe and cold-creaming her face, she propped herself up in bed with a hot-water bottle under her feet. She was reading the *Times* when the doorbell rang. At first she thought it must be a mistake and whoever it was would go away. But it rang and rang and settled to a persistent buzz. She looked at the clock: a little after eleven; it did not seem possible, she was always asleep by ten.

Climbing out of bed, she trotted barefoot across the living room. 'I'm coming, please be patient.' The latch was caught; she turned it this way and that way and the bell never paused an instant. 'Stop it,' she cried. The bolt gave way and she opened the door an inch. 'What in heaven's name?'

'Hello,' said Miriam.

'Oh... why, hello,' said Mrs Miller, stepping hesitantly into the hall. 'You're that little girl.'

'I thought you'd never answer, but I kept my finger on the button; I knew you were home. Aren't you glad to see me?'

Mrs Miller did not know what to say. Miriam, she saw, wore the same plum-velvet coat and now she had also a beret to match; her white hair was braided in two shining plaits and looped at the ends with enormous white ribbons.

'Since I've waited so long, you could at least let me in,' she said.

'It's awfully late...'

Miriam regarded her blankly. 'What difference does that make? Let me in. It's cold out here and I have on a silk dress.' Then, with a gentle gesture, she urged Mrs Miller aside and passed into the apartment.

She dropped her coat and beret on a chair. She was indeed wearing a silk dress. White silk. White silk in February. The skirt was beautifully pleated and the sleeves long; it made a faint rustle as she strolled about the room. 'I like your place,' she said. 'I like the rug, blue's my favorite color.' She touched a paper rose in a vase on the coffee table. 'Imitation,' she commented wanly. 'How sad. Aren't imitations sad?' She seated herself on the sofa, daintily spreading her skirt.

'What do you want?' asked Mrs Miller.

'Sit down,' said Miriam. 'It makes me nervous to see people stand.'

Mrs Miller sank to a hassock. 'What do you want?' she repeated.

'You know, I don't think you're glad I came.'

For a second time Mrs Miller was without an answer; her hand motioned vaguely. Miriam giggled and pressed back on a mound of chintz pillows. Mrs Miller observed that the girl was less pale than she remembered; her cheeks were flushed.

'How did you know where I lived?'

Miriam frowned. 'That's no question at all. What's your name? What's mine?'

'But I'm not listed in the phone book.'

'Oh, let's talk about something else.'

Mrs Miller said, 'Your mother must be insane to let a child like you wander around at all hours of the night – and in such ridiculous clothes. She must be out of her mind.'

Miriam got up and moved to a corner where a covered bird cage hung from a ceiling chain. She peeked beneath the cover. 'It's a canary,' she said. 'Would you mind if I woke him? I'd like to hear him sing.'

'Leave Tommy alone,' said Mrs Miller, anxiously. 'Don't you dare wake him.'

'Certainly,' said Miriam. 'But I don't see why I can't hear him sing.' And then, 'Have you anything to eat? I'm starving! Even milk and a jam sandwich would be fine.'

'Look,' said Mrs Miller, arising from the hassock, 'look – if I make some nice sandwiches will you be a good child and run along home? It's past midnight, I'm sure.'

'It's snowing,' reproached Miriam. 'And cold and dark.'

'Well, you shouldn't have come here to begin with,' said Mrs Miller, struggling to control her voice. 'I can't help the weather. If you want anything to eat you'll have to promise to leave.'

Miriam brushed a braid against her cheek. Her eyes were thoughtful, as if weighing the proposition. She turned toward the bird cage. 'Very well,' she said, 'I promise.'

How old is she? Ten? Eleven? Mrs Miller, in the kitchen, unsealed a jar of strawberry preserves and cut four slices of bread. She poured a glass of milk and paused to light a cigarette. *And why has she come?* Her hand shook as she held the match, fascinated, till it burned her finger. The canary was singing; singing as he did in the morning and at no other time. 'Miriam,' she called, 'Miriam, I told you not to disturb Tommy.' There was no answer. She called again; all she heard was the canary. She inhaled the cigarette and discovered she had lighted the cork-tip end and – oh, really, she mustn't lose her temper.

She carried the food in on a tray and set in on the coffee table. She saw first that the bird cage still wore its night cover. And

5

Tommy was singing. It gave her a queer sensation. And no one was in the room. Mrs Miller went through an alcove leading to her bedroom; at the door she caught her breath.

'What are you doing?' she asked.

Miriam glanced up and in her eyes there was a look that was not ordinary. She was standing by the bureau, a jewel case opened before her. For a minute she studied Mrs Miller, forcing their eyes to meet, and she smiled. 'There's nothing good here,' she said. 'But I like this.' Her hand held a cameo brooch. 'It's charming.'

'Suppose – perhaps you'd better put it back,' said Mrs Miller, feeling suddenly the need of some support. She leaned against the door frame; her head was unbearably heavy; a pressure weighted the rhythm of her heartbeat. The light seemed to flutter defectively. 'Please, child – a gift from my husband...'

'But it's beautiful and I want it,' said Miriam. '*Give it to me.*'

As she stood, striving to shape a sentence which would somehow save the brooch, it came to Mrs Miller there was no one to whom she might turn; she was alone; a fact that had not been among her thoughts for a long time. Its sheer emphasis was stunning. But here in her own room in the hushed snow-city were evidences she could not ignore or, she knew with startling clarity, resist.

Miriam ate ravenously, and when the sandwiches and milk were gone, her fingers made cobweb movements over the plate, gathering crumbs. The cameo gleamed on her blouse, the blonde profile like a trick reflection of its wearer. 'That was very nice,' she sighed, 'though now an almond cake or a cherry would be ideal. Sweets are lovely, don't you think?'

Mrs Miller was perched precariously on the hassock, smoking a cigarette. Her hair net had slipped lopsided and loose strands straggled down her face. Her eyes were stupidly concentrated on nothing and her cheeks were mottled in red patches, as though a fierce slap had left permanent marks.

'Is there a candy – a cake?'

Mrs Miller tapped ash on the rug. Her head swayed slightly as she tried to focus her eyes. 'You promised to leave if I made the sandwiches,' she said.

'Dear me, did I?'

'It was a promise and I'm tired and I don't feel well at all.'

'Mustn't fret,' said Miriam. 'I'm only teasing.'

She picked up her coat, slung it over her arm, and arranged her beret in front of a mirror. Presently she bent close to Mrs Miller and whispered, 'Kiss me good night.'

'Please – I'd rather not,' said Mrs Miller.

Miriam lifted a shoulder, arched an eyebrow. 'As you like,' she said, and went directly to the coffee table, seized the vase containing the paper roses, carried it to where the hard surface of the floor lay bare, and hurled it downwards. Glass sprayed in all directions and she stamped her foot on the bouquet.

Then slowly she walked to the door, but before closing it she looked back at Mrs Miller with a slyly innocent curiousity.

Mrs Miller spent the next day in bed, rising once to feed the canary and drink a cup of tea; she took her temperature and had none, yet her dreams were feverishly agitated; their unbalanced mood lingered even as she lay staring wide-eyed at the ceiling. One dream threaded through the others like an elusively mysterious theme in a complicated symphony, and the scenes it depicted were sharply outlined, as though sketched by a hand of gifted intensity: a small girl, wearing a bridal gown and a wreath of leaves, led a gray procession down a mountain path, and among them there was unusual silence till a woman at the rear asked, 'Where is she taking us?' 'No one knows,' said an old man marching in front. 'But isn't she pretty?' volunteered a third voice. 'Isn't she like a frost flower... so shining and white?'

Tuesday morning she woke up feeling better; harsh slats of sunlight, slanting through Venetian blinds, shed a disrupting light on her unwholesome fancies. She opened the window to discover a thawed, mild-as-spring day; a sweep of clean new clouds crumpled against a vastly blue, out-of-season sky; and across the low line of rooftops she could see the river and smoke curving from tugboat stacks in a warm wind. A great silver truck plowed the snow-banked street, its machine sound humming on the air.

After straightening the apartment, she went to the grocer's, cashed a check and continued to Schrafft's where she ate breakfast and chatted happily with the waitress. Oh, it was a wonderful day – more like a holiday – and it would be so foolish to go home.

She boarded a Lexington Avenue bus and rode up to Eighty-sixth Street; it was here that she had decided to do a little shopping.

She had no idea what she wanted or needed, but she idled along, intent only upon the passers-by, brisk and preoccupied, who gave her a disturbing sense of separateness.

It was while waiting at the corner of Third Avenue that she saw the man: an old man, bow-legged and stooped under an armload of bulging packages: he wore a shabby brown coat and a checkered cap. Suddenly she realized they were exchanging a smile: there was nothing friendly about this smile, it was merely two cold flickers of recognition. But she was certain she had never seen him before.

He was standing next to an El pillar, and as she crossed the street he turned and followed. He kept quite close; from the corner of her eye she watched her reflection wavering on the shopwindows.

Then in the middle of the block she stopped and faced him. He stopped also and cocked his head, grinning. But what could she say? Do? Here, in broad daylight, on Eighty-sixth Street? It was useless and, despising her own helplessness, she quickened her steps.

Now Second Avenue is a dismal street, made from scraps and ends; part cobblestone, part asphalt, part cement; and its atmosphere of desertion is permanent. Mrs Miller walked five blocks without meeting anyone, and all the while the steady crunch of his footfalls in the snow stayed near. And when she came to a florist's shop, the sound was still with her. She hurried inside and watched through the glass door as the old man passed: he kept his eyes straight ahead and didn't slow his pace, but he did one strange, telling thing: he tipped his cap.

'Six white ones, did you say? asked the florist. 'Yes,' she told him, 'white roses.' From there she went to a glassware store and selected a vase, presumably a replacement for the one Miriam had broken, though the price was intolerable and the vase itself (she thought) grotesquely vulgar. But a series of unaccountable purchases had begun, as if by prearranged plan: a plan of which she had not the least knowledge or control.

She bought a bag of glazed cherries, and at a place called the Knickerbocker Bakery she paid forty cents for six almond cakes.

Within the last hour the weather had turned cold again; like blurred lenses, winter clouds cast a shade over the sun, and the skeleton of an early dusk colored the sky; a damp mist mixed with the wind and the voices of a few children who romped high on mountains of gutter snow seemed lonely and cheerless. Soon the first flake fell, and when Mrs Miller reached the brownstone house, snow was falling in a swift screen and foot tracks vanished as they were printed.

The white roses were arranged decoratively in the vase. The glazed cherries shone on a ceramic plate. The almond cakes, dusted with sugar, awaited a hand. The canary fluttered on its swing and picked at a bar of seed.

At precisely five the doorbell rang. Mrs Miller *knew* who it was. The hem of her housecoat trailed as she crossed the floor. 'Is that you?' she called.

'Naturally,' said Miriam, the word resounding shrilly from the hall. 'Open this door.'

'Go away,' said Mrs Miller.

'Please hurry... I have a heavy package.'

'Go away,' said Mrs Miller. She returned to the living room, lighted a cigarette, sat down and calmly listened to the buzzer; on and on and on. 'You might as well leave. I have no intention of letting you in.'

Shortly the bell stopped. For possibly ten minutes Mrs Miller did not move. Then, hearing no sound, she concluded Miriam had gone. She tiptoed to the door and opened it a sliver; Miriam was half-reclining atop a cardboard box with a beautiful French doll cradled in her arms.

'Really, I thought you were never coming,' she said peevishly. 'Here, help me get this in, it's awfully heavy.'

It was not spell-like compulsion that Mrs Miller felt, but rather a curious passivity; she brought in the box, Miriam the doll. Miriam curled up on the sofa, not troubling to remove her coat or beret, and watched disinterestedly as Mrs Miller dropped the box and stood trembling, trying to catch her breath.

'Thank you,' she said. In the daylight she looked pinched and drawn, her hair less luminous. The French doll she was loving wore an exquisite powdered wig and its idiot glass eyes sought solace in Miriam's. 'I have a surprise,' she continued. 'Look into my box.'

Kneeling, Mrs Miller parted the flaps and lifted out another doll; then a blue dress which she recalled as the one Miriam had worn that first night at the theater; and of the remainder she said, 'It's all clothes. Why?'

'Because I've come to live with you,' said Miriam, twisting a cherry stem. 'Wasn't it nice of you to buy me the cherries...?'

'But you can't! For God's sake go away – go away and leave me alone!'

'...and the roses and the almond cakes? How really wonderfully generous. You know, these cherries are delicious. The last place I lived was with an old man; he was terribly poor and we never had good things to eat. But I think I'll be happy here.' She paused to snuggle her doll closer. 'Now, if you'll just show me where to put my things...'

Mrs Miller's face dissolved into a mask of ugly red lines; she began to cry, and it was an unnatural, tearless sort of weeping, as though, not having wept for a long time, she had forgotten how. Carefully she edged backward till she touched the door.

She fumbled through the hall and down the stairs to a landing below. She pounded frantically on the door of the first apartment she came to; a short, red-headed man answered and she pushed past him. 'Say, what the hell is this?' he said. 'Anything wrong, lover?' asked a young woman who appeared from the kitchen, drying her hands. And it was to her that Mrs Miller turned.

'Listen,' she cried, 'I'm ashamed behaving this way but – well, I'm Mrs H. T. Miller and I live upstairs and...' She pressed her hands over her face. 'It sounds so absurd...'

The woman guided her to a chair, while the man excitedly rattled pocket change. 'Yeah?'

'I live upstairs and there's a little girl visiting me, and I suppose that I'm afraid of her. She won't leave and I can't make her and – she's going to do something terrible. She's already stolen my cameo, but she's about to do something worse – something terrible!'

The man asked, 'Is she a relative, huh?'

Mrs Miller shook her head. 'I don't know who she is. Her name's Miriam, but I don't know for certain who she is.'

'You gotta calm down, honey,' said the woman, stroking Mrs Miller's arm. 'Harry here'll tend to this kid. Go on, lover.' And Mrs Miller said, 'The door's open – 5A.'

After the man left, the woman brought a towel and bathed Mrs Miller's face. 'You're very kind,' Mrs Miller said. 'I'm sorry to act like such a fool, only this wicked child...'

'Sure honey,' consoled the woman. 'Now, you better take it easy.'

Mrs Miller rested her head in the crook of her arm; she was quiet enough to be asleep. The woman turned a radio dial; a piano and a husky voice filled the silence and the woman, tapping her foot, kept excellent time. 'Maybe we oughta go up too,' she said.

'I don't want to see her again. I don't want to be anywhere near her.'

'Uh huh, but what you shoulda done, you shoulda called a cop.'

Presently they heard the man on the stairs. He strode into the room frowning and scratching the back of his neck. 'Nobody there,' he said, honestly embarrassed. 'She musta beat it.'

'Harry, you're a jerk,' announced the woman. 'We've been sitting here the whole time and we woulda seen...' she stopped abruptly, for the man's glance was sharp.

'I looked all over,' he said, 'and there just ain't nobody there. Nobody, understand?'

'Tell me,' said Mrs Miller, rising, 'tell me, did you see a large box? Or a doll?'

'No, ma'am, I didn't.'

And the woman, as if delivering a verdict, said, 'Well, for cryin-outloud...'

Mrs Miller entered her apartment softly; she walked to the center of the room and stood quite still. No, in a sense it had not changed: the roses, the cakes, and the cherries were in place. But this was an empty room, emptier than if the furnishings and familiars were not present, lifeless and petrified as a funeral parlor. The sofa loomed before her with a new strangeness; its vacancy had a meaning that would have been less penetrating and terrible had Miriam been curled on it. She gazed fixedly at the space where she remembered setting the box and, for a moment, the hassock spun desperately. And she looked through the window; surely the river was real, surely snow was falling – but then, one could not be certain witness to anything: Miriam, so vividly *there* and yet, where was she? Where, where?

As though moving in a dream, she sank to a chair. The room was losing shape; it was dark and getting darker and there was nothing to be done about it; she could not lift her hand to light a lamp.

Suddenly, closing her eyes, she felt an upward surge, like a diver emerging from some deeper, greener depth. In times of terror or immense distress, there are moments when the mind waits, as though for a revelation, while a skein of calm is woven over thought; it is like a sleep, or a supernatural trance; and during this lull one is aware of a force of quiet reasoning: well, what if she had never really known a girl named Miriam? that she had been foolishly frightened on the street? In the end, like everything else, it was of no importance. For the only thing she had lost to Miriam was her identity, but now she knew she had found again the person who lived in this room, who cooked her own meals, who owned a canary, who was someone she could trust and believe in: Mrs H. T. Miller.

Listening in contentment, she became aware of a double sound: a bureau drawer opening and closing; she seemed to hear it long after completion – opening and closing. Then gradually, the harshness of it was replaced by the murmur of a silk dress and this, delicately faint, was moving nearer and swelling in intensity till the walls trembled with the vibration and the room was caving under a wave of whispers. Mrs Miller stiffened and opened her eyes to a dull, direct stare.

'Hello,' said Miriam.

Thank You, M'am

Langston Hughes

She was a large woman with a large purse that had everything in it but a hammer and nails. It had a long strap, and she carried it slung across her shoulder. It was about eleven o'clock at night, dark, and she was walking alone, when a boy ran up behind her and tried to snatch her purse. The strap broke with the sudden single tug the boy gave it from behind. But the boy's weight and the weight of the purse combined caused him to lose his balance. Instead of taking off full blast as he had hoped, the boy fell on his back on the sidewalk and his legs flew up. The large woman simply turned around and kicked him right square in his blue-jeaned sitter. Then she reached down, picked the boy up by his shirt front, and shook him until his teeth rattled.

After that the woman said, 'Pick up my pocketbook, boy, and give it here.'

She still held him tightly. But she bent down enough to permit him to stoop and pick up her purse. Then she said, 'Now ain't you ashamed of yourself?'

Firmly gripped by his shirt front, the boy said, 'Yes'm.'

The woman said, 'What did you want to do it for?'

The boy said, 'I didn't aim to.'

She said, 'You a lie!'

By that time two or three people passed, stopped, turned to look, and some stood watching.

'If I turn you loose, will you run?' asked the woman.

'Yes'm,' said the boy.

'Then I won't turn you loose,' said the woman. She did not release him.

'Lady, I'm sorry,' whispered the boy.

'Um-hum! Your face is dirty. I got a great mind to wash your face for you. Ain't you got nobody home to tell you to wash your face?'

'No'm,' said the boy.

'Then it will get washed this evening,' said the large woman, starting up the street, dragging the frightened boy behind her.

He looked as if he were fourteen or fifteen, frail and willow-wild, in tennis shoes and blue jeans.

The woman said, 'You ought to be my son. I would teach you right from wrong. Least I can do right now is to wash your face. Are you hungry?'

'No'm, said the being-dragged boy. 'I just want you to turn me loose.'

'Was I bothering *you* when I turned that corner?' asked the woman.

'No'm.'

'But you put yourself in contact with *me*,' said the woman. 'If you think that contact is not going to last a while, you got another thought coming. When I get through with you, sir, you are going to remember Mrs Luella Bates Washington Jones.'

Sweat popped out on the boy's face and he began to struggle. Mrs Jones stopped, jerked him around in front of her, put a half nelson about his neck, and continued to drag him up the street. When she got to her door, she dragged the boy inside, down a hall, and into a large kitchenette-furnished room at the rear of the house. She switched on the light and left the door open. The boy could hear other roomers laughing and talking in the large house. Some of their doors were open, too, so he knew he and the woman were not alone. The woman still had him by the neck in the middle of her room.

'She said, 'What is your name?'

'Roger,' answered the boy.

'Then, Roger, you go to that sink and wash your face,' said the woman, whereupon she turned him loose – at last. Roger looked at the door – looked at the woman – looked at the door – *and went to the sink.*

'Let the water run until it gets warm,' she said. 'Here's a clean towel.'

'You gonna take me to jail?' asked the boy, bending over the sink.

'Not with that face, I would not take you nowhere,' said the woman. 'Here I am trying to get home to cook me a bite to eat, and you snatch my pocketbook! Maybe you ain't been to your supper either, late as it be. Have you?'

'There's nobody home at my house,' said the boy.

'Then we'll eat,' said the woman. 'I believe you're hungry – or been hungry – to try to snatch my pocketbook!'

'I want a pair of blue suede shoes,' said the boy.

'Well, you didn't have to snatch *my* pocketbook to get some suede shoes,' said Mrs Luella Bates Washington Jones. 'You could of asked me.'

'M'am?'

The water dripping from his face, the boy looked at her. There was a long pause. A very long pause. After he had dried his face, and not knowing what else to do, dried it again, the boy turned around, wondering what next. The door was open. He could make a dash for it down the hall. He could run, run, run, *run!*

The woman was sitting on the daybed. After a while she said, 'I were young once and I wanted things I could not get.'

There was another long pause. The boy's mouth opened. Then he frowned, not knowing he frowned.

The woman said, 'Um-hum! You thought I was going to say *but*, didn't you? You thought I was going to say, *but I didn't snatch people's pocketbooks*. Well, I wasn't going to say that,' Pause. Silence. 'I have done things, too, which I would not tell you, son – neither tell God, if He didn't already know. Everybody's got something in common. So you set down while I fix us something to eat. You might run that comb through your hair so you will look presentable.'

In another corner of the room behind a screen was a gas plate and an icebox. Mrs Jones got up and and went behind the screen. The woman did not watch the boy to see if he was going to run now, nor did she watch her purse, which she left behind her on the daybed. But the boy took care to sit on the far side of the room, away from the purse, where he thought she could easily see him out of the corner of her eye if she wanted to. He did not trust the woman *not* to trust him. And he did not want to be mistrusted now.

'Do you need somebody to go to the store,' asked the boy, 'maybe to get some milk or something?'

'Don't believe I do,' said the woman, 'unless you just want sweet milk yourself. I was going to make some cocoa out of this canned milk I got here.'

'That will be fine,' said the boy.

She heated some lima beans and ham she had in the icebox, made the cocoa, and set the table. The woman did not ask the boy anything about where he lived, or his folks, or anything else that would embarrass him. Instead, as they ate, she told him about her job in a hotel beauty shop that stayed open late, what the work was like, and how all kinds of women came in and out, blonds, redheads, and Spanish. Then she cut him a half of her ten-cent cake.

'Eat some more, son,' she said.

When they were finished eating, she got up and said, 'Now here, take this ten dollars and buy yourself some blue suede shoes. And next time, do not make the mistake of latching onto *my* pocketbook *nor nobody else's* – because shoes got by devilish ways will burn your feet. I got to get my rest now. But from here on in, son, I hope you will behave yourself.'

She led him down the hall to the front door and opened it. 'Good night! Behave yourself, boy!' she said, looking out into the street as he went down the steps.

The boy wanted to say something other than, 'Thank you, M'am,' to Mrs Luella Bates Washington Jones, but although his lips moved, he couldn't even say that as he turned at the foot of the barren stoop and looked up at the large woman in the door. Then she shut the door.

Breakfast

John Steinbeck

This thing fills me with pleasure. I don't know why, I can see it in the smallest detail. I find myself recalling it again and again, each time bringing more detail out of a sunken memory, remembering brings the curious warm pleasure.

It was very early in the morning. The eastern mountains were black-blue, but behind them the light stood up faintly colored at the mountain rims with a washed red, growing colder, grayer and darker as it went up and overhead until, at a place near the west, it merged with pure night.

And it was cold, not painfully so, but cold enough so that I rubbed my hands and shoved them deep into my pockets and I hunched my shoulders up and scuffled my feet on the ground. Down in the valley where I was, the earth was that lavender gray of dawn. I walked along a country road and ahead of me I saw a tent that was only a little lighter gray than the ground. Beside the tent there was a flash of orange fire seeping out of the cracks of an old, rusty, iron stove. Gray smoke spurted up out of the stubby stovepipe, spurted up a long way before it spread out and dissipated.

I saw a young woman beside the stove, really a girl. She was dressed in a faded cotton skirt and waist. As I came close I saw that she carried a baby in a crooked arm and the baby was nursing, its head under her waist out of the cold. The mother moved about, poking the fire, shifting the rusty lids of the stove to make a greater draught, opening the oven door; and all the time the baby was nursing, but that didn't interfere with the mother's work, nor with the light quick gracefulness of her movements. There was something very precise and practiced in her movements. The orange fire flicked out of the cracks in the stove and threw dancing reflections on the tent.

I was close now and I could smell frying bacon and baking bread, the warmest, pleasantest odors I know. From the east the light grew swiftly. I came near to the stove and stretched my hands out to it and shivered all over when the warmth struck me. Then the tent-flap jerked up and a young man came out and an older man followed him. They were dressed in new blue dungarees and in new dungaree coats with the brass buttons shining. They were sharp-faced men, and they looked much alike.

The younger had a dark stubble beard and the older had a gray stubble beard. Their heads and faces were wet, their hair dripped with water, and water stood out on their stiff beards and their cheeks shone with water. Together they stood looking quietly at the lightening east; they yawned together and looked at the light on the hill rims. They turned and saw me.

'Morning,' said the older man. His face was neither friendly nor unfriendly.

'Morning, sir,' I said.

'Morning,' said the young man.

The water was slowly drying on their faces. They came to the stove and warmed their hands at it.

The girl kept to her work, her face averted and her eyes on what she was doing. Her hair was tied back out of her eyes with a string and it hung down her back and swayed as she worked. She set tin cups on a big packing-box, set tin plates and knives and forks out too. Then she scooped fried bacon out of the deep grease and laid it on a big tin platter, and the bacon cricked and rustled as it grew crisp. She opened the rusty oven door and took out a square pan full of high big biscuits.

When the smell of that hot bread came out, both of the men inhaled deeply. The young man said softly: 'Keerist!'

The elder man turned to me: 'Had your breakfast?'

'No.'

'Well, sit down with us, then.'

That was the signal. We went to the packing-case and squatted on the ground about it. The young man asked: 'Picking cotton?'

'No.'

'We had twelve days' work so far,' the young man said.

The girl spoke from the stove. 'They even got new clothes.'

The two men looked down at their new dungarees and they both smiled a little.

The girl set out the platter of bacon, the brown high biscuits, a bowl of bacon gravy and a pot of coffee, and then she squatted down by the box too. The baby was still nursing, its head up under her waist out of the cold. I could hear the sucking noises it made.

We filled our plates, poured bacon gravy over our biscuits and sugared our coffee. The older man filled his mouth full and he chewed and chewed and swallowed. Then he said: 'God Almighty, it's good,' and he filled his mouth again.

The young man said: 'We been eating good for twelve days.'

We all ate quickly, frantically, and refilled our plates and ate quickly again until we were full and warm. The hot bitter coffee scalded our throats. We threw the last little bits with the grounds in it on the earth and refilled our cups.

There was color in the light now, a reddish gleam that made the air seem colder. The two men faced the east and their faces were lighted by the dawn, and I looked up for a moment and saw the image of the mountain and the light coming over it reflected in the older man's eyes.

Then the two men threw the grounds from their cups on the earth and they stood up together. 'Got to get going,' the older man said.

The younger turned to me. ''Fyou want to pick cotton, we could maybe get you on.'

'No. I got to go along. Thanks for breakfast.'

The older man waved his hand in a negative. 'O.K. Glad to have you.' They walked away together. The air was blazing with light at the eastern skyline. And I walked away down the country road.

That's all. I know, of course, some of the reasons why it was pleasant. But there was some element of great beauty there that makes the rush of warmth when I think of it.

Superman and Paula Brown's New Snowsuit

Sylvia Plath

The year the war began I was in the fifth grade at the Annie F. Warren Grammar School in Winthrop, and that was the winter I won the prize for drawing the best Civil Defense signs. That was also the winter of Paula Brown's new snowsuit, and even now, thirteen years later, I can recall the changing colors of those days, clear and definite as patterns seen through a kaleidoscope.

I lived on the bay side of town, on Johnson Avenue, opposite the Logan Airport, and before I went to bed each night, I used to kneel by the west window of my room and look over to the lights of Boston that blazed and blinked far off across the darkening water. The sunset flaunted its pink flag above the airport, and the sound of waves was lost in the perpetual droning of the planes. I marveled at the moving beacons on the runway and watched, until it grew completely dark, the flashing red and green lights that rose and set in the sky like shooting stars. The airport was my Mecca, my Jerusalem. All night I dreamed of flying.

Those were the days of my technicolor dreams. Mother believed that I should have an enormous amount of sleep, and so I was never really tired when I went to bed. This was the best time of the day, when I could lie in the vague twilight, drifting off to sleep, making up dreams inside my head the way they should go. My flying dreams were believable as a landscape by Dali, so real that I would awake with a sudden shock, a breathless sense of having tumbled like Icarus from the sky and caught myself on the soft bed just in time.

These nightly adventures in space began when Superman started invading my dreams and teaching me how to fly. He used to come roaring by in his shining blue suit with his cape whistling in the wind, looking remarkably like my Uncle Frank who was living with Mother and me. In the magic whirring of his cape I could hear the wings of a hundred seagulls, the motors of a thousand planes.

I was not the only worshipper of Superman in our block. David Sterling, a pale, bookish boy who lived down the street, shared my love for the sheer poetry of flight. Before supper every night, we listened to Superman together on the radio, and during the day we made up our own adventures on the way to school.

The Annie F. Warren Grammar School was a red brick building, set back from the main highway on a black tar street, surrounded by barren gravel playgrounds. Out by the parking lot David and I found a perfect alcove for our Superman dramas. The dingy back entrance to the school was deep set in a long passageway which was an excellent place for surprise captures and sudden rescues.

During recess, David and I came into our own. We ignored the boys playing baseball on the gravel court and the girls giggling at dodge-ball in the dell. Our Superman games made us outlaws, yet gave us a sense of windy superiority. We even found a stand-in for a villain in Sheldon Fein, the sallow mamma's boy on our block who was left out of the boy's games because he cried whever anybody tagged him and always managed to fall down and skin his fat knees.

At first, we had to prompt Sheldon in his part, but after a while he became an expert on inventing tortures and even carried them out in private, beyond the game. He used to pull the wings from flies and the legs off grasshoppers, and keep the broken insects captive in a jar hidden under his bed where he could take them out in secret and watch them struggling. David and I never played with Sheldon except at recess. After school we left him to his mamma, his bonbons, and his helpless insects.

At this time my Uncle Frank was living with us while waiting to be drafted, and I was sure that he bore an extraordinary resemblance to Superman incognito. David couldn't see his likeness as clearly as I did, but he admitted that Uncle Frank was the strongest man he had ever known, and he could do lots of tricks like making caramels disappear under napkins and walking on his hands.

That same winter, war was declared, and I remember sitting by the radio with Mother and Uncle Frank and feeling a queer foreboding in the air. Their voices were low and serious, and their talk was of planes and German bombs. Uncle Frank said something about Germans in America being put in prison for the duration, and Mother kept saying over and over again about Daddy: 'I'm only glad Otto didn't live to see this; I'm only glad Otto didn't live to see it come to this.'

In school we began to draw Civil Defense signs, and that was when I beat Jimmy Lane in our block for the fifth grade prize. Every now and then we would practice an air raid. The fire bell would ring and we would take up our coats and pencils and file down the creaking stairs to the basement where we sat in special corners according to our color tags, and put the pencils between out teeth so the bombs wouldn't make us bite our tongues by mistake. Some of the little children in the lower grades would cry because it was dark in the cellar, with only the bare ceiling lights on the cold black stone.

The threat of war was seeping in everywhere. At recess, Sheldon became a Nazi and borrowed a goose-step from the movies, but his Uncle Macy was really over in Germany, and Mrs Fein began to grow thin and pale because she heard that Macy was a prisoner and then nothing more.

The winter dragged on, with a wet east wind coming always from the ocean, and the snow melting before there was enough for coasting. One Friday afternoon, just before Christmas, Paula Brown gave her annual birthday party, and I was invited because it was for all the children on our block. Paula lived across from Jimmy Lane on Somerset Terrace, and nobody on our block really liked her because she was bossy and stuck-up, with pale skin and long red pigtails and watery blue eyes.

She met us at the door of her house in a white organdy dress, her red hair tied up in sausage curls with a satin bow. Before we could sit down at the table for birthday cake and ice-cream, she had to show us all her presents. There were a great many because it was both her birthday and Christmas time too.

Paula's favorite present was a new snowsuit, and she tried it on for us. The snowsuit was powder blue and came in a silver box from Sweden, she said. The front of the jacket was all embroidered with pink and white roses and bluebirds, and the leggings had embroidered straps. She even had a little white angora beret and angora mittens to go with it.

After dessert we were all driven to the movies by Jimmy Lane's father to see the late afternoon show as a special treat. Mother had found out that the main feature was *Snow White* before she would let me go, but she hadn't realized that there was a war picture playing with it.

The movie was about Japanese prisoners who were being tortured by having no food or water. Our war games and the radio programs were all made up, but this was real, this really happened. I blocked my ears to shut out the groans of the thirsty, starving men, but I could not tear my eyes away from the screen.

Finally, the prisoners pulled down a heavy log from the log rafters and jammed it through the clay wall so they could reach the fountain in the court, but just as the first man got to the water, the Japanese began shooting the prisoners dead, and stamping on them, and laughing. I was sitting on the aisle, and I stood up then in a hurry and ran out to the girls' room where I knelt over a toilet bowl and vomited up the cake and ice cream.

After I went to bed that night, as soon as I closed my eyes, the prison camp sprang to life in my mind, and again the groaning men broke through the walls, and again they were shot down as they reached the trickling fountain. No matter how hard I thought of Superman before I went to sleep, no crusading blue figure came roaring down in heavenly anger to smash the yellow men who invaded my dreams. When I woke up in the morning, my sheets were damp with sweat.

Saturday was bitterly cold, and the skies were gray and blurred with the threat of snow. I was dallying home from the store that afternoon, curling up my chilled fingers in my mittens, when I saw a couple of kids playing Chinese tag out in front of Paula Brown's house.

Paula stopped in the middle of the game to eye me coldly. 'We need someone else,' she said. 'Want to play?' she tagged me on the ankle then, and I hopped around and finally caught Sheldon Fein as he was bending down to fasten one of his furlined overshoes. An early thaw had melted away the snow in the street, and the tarred pavement was gritted with sand left from the snow trucks. In front of Paula's house somebody's car had left a glittering black stain of oil slick.

We went running about in the street, retreating to the hard, brown lawns when the one who was 'It' came too close. Jimmy Lane came out of his house and stood watching us for a short while, and then joined in. Every time he was 'It', he chased Paula in her powder blue snowsuit, and she screamed shrilly and looked around at him with her wide, watery eyes, and he always managed to catch her.

Only one time she forgot to look where she was going, and as Jimmy reached out to tag her, she slid into the oil slick. We all froze when she went down on her side as if we were playing statues. No one said a word, and for a minute there was only the sound of the planes across the bay. The dull, green light of late afternoon came closing down on us, cold and final as a window blind.

Paula's snowsuit was smeared wet and black with oil along the side. Her angora mittens were dripping like black cat's fur. Slowly, she sat up and looked at us standing around her, as if searching for something. Then, suddenly, her eyes fixed on me.

'You,' she said deliberately, pointing at me, 'you pushed me.'

There was another second of silence, and then Jimmy Lane turned on me, 'You did it,' he taunted. 'You did it.'

Sheldon and Paula and Jimmy and the rest of them faced me with a strange joy flickering in the back of their eyes. 'You did it, you pushed her,' they said.

And even when I shouted 'I did not!' they were all moving in on me, chanting in a chorus, 'Yes, you did, yes, you did, we saw you.' In the well of faces moving toward me I saw no help, and I

25

began to wonder if Jimmy had pushed Paula, or if she had fallen by herself, and I was not sure. I wasn't sure at all.

I started walking past them, walking home, determined not to run, but when I had left them behind me, I felt the sharp thud of a snowball on my left shoulder, and another. I picked up a faster stride and rounded the corner by Kelly's. There was my dark brown shingled house ahead of me, and inside, Mother and Uncle Frank, home on furlough. I began to run in the cold, raw evening toward the bright squares of light in the windows that were home.

Uncle Frank met me at the door. 'How's my favorite trooper?' he asked, and he swung me so high in the air that my head grazed the ceiling. There was a big love in his voice that drowned out the shouting which still echoed in my ears.

'I'm fine,' I lied, and he taught me some jujitsu in the living room until Mother called us for supper.

Candles were set on the white linen tablecloth, and miniature flames flickered in the silver and the glasses. I could see another room reflected beyond the dark dining-room window where the people laughed and talked in a secure web of light, held together by its indestructible brilliance.

All at once the doorbell rang, and Mother rose to answer it. I could hear David Sterling's high, clear voice in the hall. There was a cold draft from the open doorway, but he and Mother kept on talking, and he did not come in. When Mother came back to the table, her face was sad. 'Why didn't you tell me?' she said, 'why didn't you tell me that you pushed Paula in the mud and spoiled her new snowsuit?'

A mouthful of chocolate pudding blocked my throat, thick and bitter. I had to wash it down with milk. Finally I said, 'I didn't do it.'

But the words came out like hard, dry little seeds, hollow and insincere. I tried again. 'I didn't do it. Jimmy Lane did it.'

'Of course we'll believe you,' Mother said slowly, 'but the whole neighborhood is talking about it. Mrs Sterling heard the story from Mrs Fein and sent David over to say we should buy Paula a new snowsuit. I can't understand it.'

'I didn't do it,' I repeated, and the blood beat in my ears like a slack drum. I pushed my chair away from the table, not looking at Uncle Frank or Mother sitting there, solemn and sorrowful in the candlelight.

The staircase to the second floor was dark, but I went down to the long hall to my room without turning on the light switch and shut the door. A small unripe moon was shafting squares of greenish light along the floor and the windowpanes were fringed with frost.

I threw myself fiercely down on my bed and lay there, dry-eyed and burning. After a while I heard Uncle Frank coming up the stairs and knocking on my door. When I didn't answer, he walked in and sat down on my bed. I could see his strong shoulders bulk against the moonlight, but in the shadows his face was featureless.

'Tell me, Honey,' he said very softly, 'tell me. You don't have to be afraid. We'll understand. Only tell me what really happened. You have never had to hide anything from me, you know that. Only tell me how it really happened.'

'I told you,' I said. 'I told you what happened, and I can't make it any different. Not even for you I can't make it any different.'

He sighed then and got up to go away. 'Okay, Honey,' he said at the door. 'Okay, but we'll pay for another snowsuit anyway just to make everybody happy, and ten years from now no one will ever know the difference.'

The door shut behind him and I could hear his footsteps growing fainter as he walked off down the hall. I lay there alone in bed, feeling the black shadow creeping up the underside of the world like a flood tide. Nothing held, nothing was left. The silver airplanes and the blue capes all dissolved and vanished, wiped away like the crude drawings of a child in colored chalk from the colossal blackboard of the dark. That was the year the war began, and the real world, and the difference.

Sweat

Zora Neale Hurston

It was eleven o'clock of a Spring night in Florida. It was Sunday. Any other night, Delia Jones would have been in bed for two hours by this time. But she was a washwoman, and Monday morning meant a great deal to her. So she collected the soiled clothes on Saturday when she returned the clean things. Sunday night after church, she sorted them and put the white things to soak. It saved her almost a half day's start. A great hamper in the bedroom held the clothes that she brought home. It was so much neater than a number of bundles lying around.

She squatted in the kitchen floor beside the great pile of clothes, sorting them into heaps according to color, and humming a song in a mournful key, but wondering through it all where Sykes, her husband, had gone with her horse and buckboard.

Just then something long, round, limp and black fell upon her shoulders and slithered to the floor beside her. A great terror took hold of her. It softened her knees and dried her mouth so that it was a full minute before she could cry out or move. Then she saw that it was the big bull whip her husband liked to carry when he drove.

She lifted her eyes to the door and saw him standing there bent over with laughter at her fright. She screamed at him.

'Sykes, what you throw dat whip on me like dat? You know it would skeer me – looks just like a snake, an' you know how skeered Ah is of snakes.'

'Course Ah knowed it! That's how come Ah done it.' He slapped his leg with his hand and almost rolled on the ground in his mirth. 'If you such a big fool dat you got to have a fit over a earth worm or a string, Ah don't keer how bad Ah skeer you.'

'You ain't got no business doing it. Gawd knows it's a sin. Some day Ah'm gointuh drop dead from some of yo' foolishness.

'Nother thing, where you been wid mah rig? Ah feeds dat pony. He ain't fuh you to be drivin' wid no bull whip.'

'You sho is one aggravatin' nigger woman!' he declared and stepped into the room. She resumed her work and did not answer him at once. 'Ah done tole you time and again to keep them white folks' clothes outa dis house.'

He picked up the whip and glared down at her. Delia went on with her work. She went out into the yard and returned with a galvanized tub and set it on the washbench. She saw that Sykes had kicked all of the clothes together again, and now stood in her way truculently, his whole manner hoping, *praying*, for an argument. But she walked calmly around him and commenced to re-sort the things.

'Next time, Ah'm gointer kick 'em outdoors,' he threatened as he struck a match along the leg of his corduroy breeches.

Delia never looked up from her work, and her thin, stooped shoulders sagged further.

'Ah ain't for no fuss t'night Sykes. Ah just come from taking sacrament at the church house.'

He snorted scornfully. 'Yeah, you just come from de church house on a Sunday night, but heah you is gone to work on them clothes. You ain't nothing but a hypocrite. One of them amen-corner Christians – sing, whoop, and shout, then come home and wash white folks' clothes on the Sabbath.'

He stepped roughly upon the whitest pile of things, kicking them helter-skelter as he crossed the room. His wife gave a little scream of dismay, and quickly gathered them together again.

'Sykes, you quit grindin' dirt into these clothes! How can Ah git through by Sat'day if Ah don't start on Sunday?'

'Ah don't keer if you never git through. Anyhow, Ah done promised Gawd and a couple of other men, Ah ain't gointer have it in mah house. Don't gimme no lip neither, else Ah'll throw 'em out and put mah fist up side yo' head to boot.'

Delia's habitual meekness seemed to slip from her shoulders like a blown scarf. She was on her feet, her poor little body, her bare knuckly hands bravely defying the strapping hulk before her.

'Looka heah, Sykes, you done gone too fur. Ah been married to you fur fifteen years, and Ah been takin' in washin' fur fifteen years. Sweat, sweat, sweat! Work and sweat, cry and sweat, pray and sweat!'

'What's that got to do with me?' he asked brutally.

'What's it got to do with you, Sykes? Mah tub of suds is filled yo' belly with vittles more times than yo' hands is filled it. Mah sweat is done paid for this house and Ah reckon Ah kin keep on sweatin' in it.'

She seized the iron skillet from the stove and struck a defensive pose, which act surprised him greatly, coming from her. It cowed him and he did not strike her as he usually did.

'Naw you won't,' she panted, 'that ole snaggle-toothed black woman you runnin' with ain't comin' heah to pile up on *mah* sweat and blood. You ain't paid for nothin' on this place, and Ah'm gointer stay right heah till Ah'm toted out foot foremost.'

'Well, you better quit gittin' me riled up, else they'll be totin' you out sooner than you expect. Ah'm so tired of you Ah don't know whut to do. Gawd! how Ah hates skinny wimmen!'

A little awed by this new Delia, he sidled out of the door and slammed the back gate after him. He did not say where he had gone, but she knew too well. She knew very well that he would not return until nearly daybreak also. Her work over, she went on to bed but did not sleep at once. Things had come to a pretty pass!

She lay awake, gazing upon the debris that cluttered their matrimonial trail. Not an image left standing along the way. Anything like flowers had long ago been drowned in the salty stream that had been pressed from her heart. Her tears, her sweat, her blood. She had brought love to the union and he had brought a longing after the flesh. Two months after the wedding, he had given her the first brutal beating. She had the memory of his numerous trips to Orlando with all of his wages when he had returned to her penniless, even before the first year had passed. She was young and soft then, but now she thought of her knotty, muscled limbs, her harsh knuckly hands, and drew herself up into an unhappy little ball in the middle of the big feather bed.

Too late now to hope for love, even if it were not Bertha it would be someone else. This case differed from the others only in that she was bolder than the others. Too late for everything except her little home. She had built it for her old days, and planted one by one the trees and flowers there. It was lovely to her, lovely.

Somehow, before sleep came, she found herself saying aloud: 'Oh well, whatever goes over the Devil's back, is got to come under his belly. Sometime or ruther, Sykes, like everybody else, is gointer reap his sowing.' After that she was able to build a spiritual earthworks against her husband. His shells could no longer reach her. *Amen.* She went to sleep and slept until he announced his presence in bed by kicking her feet and rudely snatching the covers away.

'Gimme some kivah heah, an' git yo' damn foots over on yo' own side! Ah oughter mash you in yo' mouf fuh drawing dat skillet on me.'

Delia went clear to the rail without answering him. A triumphant indifference to all that he was or did.

The week was as full of work for Delia as all other weeks, and Saturday found her behind her little pony, collecting and delivering clothes.

It was a hot, hot day near the end of July. The village men on Joe Clarke's porch even chewed cane listlessly. They did not hurl the caneknots as usual. They let them dribble over the edge of the porch. Even conversation had collapsed under the heat.

'Heah come Delia Jones,' Jim Merchant said, as the shaggy pony came 'round the bend of the road toward them. The rusty buckboard was heaped with baskets of crisp, clean laundry.

'Yep,' Joe Lindsay agreed. 'Hot or col', rain or shine, jes ez reg'lar ez de weeks roll roun' Delia carries 'em an' fetches 'em on Sat'day.'

'She better if she wanter eat,' said Moss. 'Syke Jones ain't wuth de shot an' powder hit would tek tuh kill 'em. Not to *huh* he ain't.'

'He sho' ain't,' Walter Thomas chimed in. 'It's too bad, too, cause she wuz a right pritty lil trick when he got huh. Ah'd uh mah'ied huh mahseff if he hadnter beat me to it.'

Delia nodded briefly at the men as she drove past.

'Too much knockin' will ruin *any* 'oman. He done beat huh 'nough tuh kill three women, let 'lone change they looks,' said Elijah Moseley. 'How Syke kin stommuck dat big black greasy Mogul he's layin' roun' wid, gits me. Ah swear dat eight-rock couldn't kiss a sardine can Ah done thowed out de back do' 'way las' yeah.'

'Aw, she's fat, thass how come. He's allus been crazy 'bout fat women,' put in Merchant. 'He'd a' been tied up wid one long time ago if he could a' found one tuh have him. Did Ah tell you 'bout him come sidlin' roun' *mah* wife – bringin' her a basket uh peecans outa his yard fuh a present? Yessir, ma wife! She tol' him tuh take 'em right straight back home, cause Delia works so hard ovah dat washtub she reckon everything on de place taste lak sweat an' soapsuds. Ah jus' wisht Ah'd a' caught 'im 'roun' dere! Ah'd a' made his hips ketch on fiah down dat shell road.'

'Ah know he done it, too. Ah sees 'im grinnin' at every 'oman dat passes,' Walter Thomas said. 'But even so, he useter eat some mighty big hunks uh humble pie tuh git dat lil' 'oman he got. She wuz ez pritty ez a speckled pup! Dat wuz fifteen yeahs ago. He useter be so skeered uh losin' huh, she could make him do some parts of a husband's duty. Dey never wiz de same in de mind.'

'There oughter be a law about him,' said Lindsay. 'He ain't fit tuh carry guts tuh a bear.'

Clarke spoke for the first time. 'Taint no law on earth dat kin make a man be decent if it aint in 'im. There's plenty men dat takes a wife lak dey do a joint uh sugar-cane. It's round, juicy an' sweet when dey gits it. But dey squeeze an' grind, squeeze an' grind an' wring tell dey wring every drop uh pleasure dat's in 'em out. When dey's satisfied dat dey is wrung dry, dey treats 'em jes lak dey do a cane-chew. Dey throws 'em away. Dey knows whut dey is doin' while dey is at it, an' hates theirselves fuh it but they keeps on hangin' after huh tell she's empty. Den dey hates huh fuh bein' a cane-chew an' in de way.'

'We oughter take Syke an' dat 'oman un his'n down in Lake Howell swamp an' lay on de rawhide till they cain't say Lawd a' mussy. He allus wuz uh ovahbearin' niggah, but since dat white 'oman from up north done teached 'im how to run a automobile, he done got too biggety to live – an' we oughter kill 'im,' Old Man Anderson advised.

A grunt of approval went around the porch. But the heat was melting their civic virtue and Elijah Moseley began to bait Joe Clarke.

'Come on, Joe, git a melon outa dere an' slice it up for yo' customers. We'se all sufferin' wid de heat. De bear's done got *me!'*

'Thass right, Joe, a watermelon is jes' whut Ah needs tuh cure de eppizudicks,' Walter Thomas joined forces with Moseley. 'Come on dere, Joe. We all is steady customers an' you aint set us up in a long time. Ah chooses dat long, bowlegged Floridy favorite.'

'A god, an' be dough. You all gimme twenty cents and slice way.' Clarke retorted. 'Ah needs a col' slice m'self. Heah, everybody chip in. Ah'll lend y'll mah meat knife.'

The money was quickly subscribed and the huge melon brought forth. At that moment, Sykes and Bertha arrived. A determined silence fell on the porch and the melon was put away again.

Merchant snapped down the blade of his jackknife and moved toward the store door.

'Come on in, Joe, an' gimme a slab uh sow belly an' uh pound uh coffee – almost fuhgot 'twas Sat'day. Got to git on home.' Most of the men left also.

Just then Delia drove past on her way home, as Sykes was ordering magnificently for Bertha. It pleased him for Delia to see.

'Git whutsoever yo' heart desires, Honey. Wait a minute, Joe. Give huh two botles uh strawberry soda-water, uh quart uh parched groundpeas, an' a block uh chewin' gum.'

With all this they left the store, with Sykes reminding Bertha that this was his town and she could have it if she wanted it.

The men returned soon after they left, and held their watermelon feast.

'Where did Syke Jones git da 'oman from nohow?' Lindsay asked.

'Ovah Apopka. Guess dey musta been cleanin' out de town when she lef'. She don't look lak a thing but a hunk uh liver wid hair on it.'

'Well, she sho' kin squall,' Dave Carter contributed. 'When she gits ready tuh laff, she jes' opens huh mouf an' latches it back tuh de las' notch. No ole grandpa alligator down in Lake Bell ain't got nothin' on huh.'

Bertha had been in town three months now. Sykes was still paying her room rent at Della Lewis' – the only house in town that would have taken her in. Sykes took her frequently to Winter Park to 'stomps.' He still assured her that he was the swellest man in the state.

'Sho' you kin have dat lil' ole house soon's Ah kin git dat 'oman outa dere. Everything b'longs tuh me an' you sho' kin have it. Ah sho' 'bominates uh skinny 'oman. Lawdy, you sho' is got one portly shape on you! You kin git *anything* you wants. Dis is *mah* town an' you sho' kin have it.'

Delia's work-worn knees crawled over the earth in Gethsemane and up the rocks of Calvary many, many times during these months. She avoided the villagers and meeting places in her efforts to be blind and deaf. But Bertha nullified this to a degree, by coming to Delia's house to call Sykes out to her at the gate.

Delia and Sykes fought all the time now with no peaceful interludes. They slept and ate in silence. Two or three times Delia had attempted a timid friendliness, but she was repulsed each time. It was plain that the breaches must remain agape.

The sun had burned July to August. The heat streamed down like a million hot arrows, smiting all things living upon the earth. Grass withered, leaves browned, snakes went blind in shedding and men and dogs went mad. Dog days!

Delia came home one day and found Sykes there before her. She wondered, but started to go on into the house without speaking, even though he was standing in the kitchen door and she must either stoop under his arm or ask him to move. He made no room for her. She noticed a soap box beside the steps, but paid no particular attention to it, knowing that he must have brought it there. As she was stooping to pass under his outstretched arm, he suddenly pushed her backward, laughingly.

'Look in de box dere Delia, Ah done brung yuh somethin'!'

She nearly fell upon the box in her stumbling, and when she saw what it held, she all but fainted outright.

'Syke! Syke, mah Gawd! You take dat rattlesnake 'way from heah! You *gottuh*. Oh, Jesus, have mussy!'

'Ah ain't gut tuh do nuthin' uh de kin' – fact is Ah ain't got tuh do nothin' but die. Taint no use uh you puttin' on airs makin' out lak you skeered uh dat snake – he's gointer stay right heah tell he die. He wouldn't bite me cause Ah knows how tuh handle 'im. Nohow he wouldn't risk breakin' out his fangs 'gin *yo'* skinny laigs.'

'Naw, now Syke, don't keep dat thing 'roun' heah tuh skeer me tuh death. You knows Ah'm even feared uh earth worms. Thass de biggest snake Ah evah did see. Kill 'im Syke, please.'

'Doan ast me tuh do nothin' fuh yuh. Goin' roun' tryin' tuh be so damp asterperious. Naw, Ah ain't gonna kill it. Ah think uh damn sight mo' uh him dan you! Dat's a nice snake an' anybody doan lak 'im kin jes' hit de grit.'

The village soon heard that Sykes had the snake, and came to see and ask questions.

'How de hen-fire did you ketch dat six-foot rattler, Syke?' Thomas asked.

'He's full uh frogs so he cain't hardly move, thass how Ah eased up on 'm. But Ah'm a snake charmer an' knows how tuh handle 'em. Shux, dat ain't nothin'. Ah could ketch one eve'y day if Ah so wanted tuh.'

'Whut he needs is a heavy hick'ry club leaned real heavy on his head. Dat's de bes 'way tuh charm a rattlesnake.'

'Naw, Walt, y'll jes' don't understand dese diamon' backs lak Ah do,' said Sykes in a superior tone of voice.

The village agreed with Walter, but the snake stayed on. His box remained by the kitchen door with its screen wire covering.

Two or three days later it had digested its meal of frogs and literally came to life. It rattled at every movement in the kitchen or the yard. One day as Delia came down the kitchen steps she saw his chalky-white fangs curved like scimitars hung in the wire meshes. This time she did not run away with averted eyes as usual. She stood for a long time in the doorway in a red fury that grew bloodier for every second that she regarded the creature that was her torment.

That night she broached the subject as soon as Sykes sat down to the table.

'Syke, Ah wants you tuh take dat snake 'way fum heah. You done starved me an' Ah put up widcher, you done beat me an Ah took dat, but you done kilt all mah insides bringin' dat varmint heah.'

Sykes poured out a saucer full of coffee and drank it deliberately before he answered her.

'A whole lot Ah keer 'bout how you feels inside uh out. Dat snake ain't goin' no damn wheah till Ah gits ready fuh 'im tuh go. So fur as beatin' is concerned, yuh ain't took near all dat you gointer take ef yuh stay 'roun' *me*.'

Delia pushed back her plate and got up from the table. 'Ah hates you, Sykes,' she said calmly. 'Ah hates you tuh de same degree dat Ah useter love yuh. Ah done took an' took till mah belly is full up tuh mah neck. Dat's de reason Ah got mah letter fum de church an' moved mah membership tuh Woodbridge – so Ah don't haftuh take no sacrament wid yuh. Ah don't wantuh see yuh 'roun' me atall. Lay 'roun' wid dat 'oman all yuh wants tuh, but gwan 'way fum me an' mah house. Ah hates yuh lak uh suck-egg dog.'

Sykes almost let the huge wad of corn bread and collard greens he was chewing fall out of his mouth in amazement. He had a hard time whipping himself up to the proper fury to try to answer Delia.

'Well, Ah'm glad you does hate me. Ah'm sho' tiahed uh you hangin' ontuh me. Ah don't want yuh. Look at yuh stringey ole neck! Yo' rawbony laigs an' arms is enough tuh cut uh man tuh death. You looks jes' lak de devvul's doll-baby tuh *me*. You cain't hate me no worse dan Ah hates you. Ah been hatin' *you* fuh years.'

'Yo' ole black hide don't look lak nothin' tuh me, but uh passle uh wrinkled up rubber, wid yo' big ole yeahs flappin' on each side lak uh paih uh buzzard wings. Don't think Ah'm gointuh be run 'way fum mah house neither. Ah'm goin' tuh de white folks bout *you*, mah young man, de very nex' time you lay yo' han's on me. Mah cup is done run ovah.' Delia said this with no signs of fear and Sykes departed from the house, threatening her, but made not the slightest move to carry out any of them.

That night he did not return at all, and the next day being Sunday, Delia was glad she did not have to quarrel before she hitched up her pony and drove the four miles to Woodbridge.

She stayed to the night service – 'love feast' – which was very warm and full of spirit. In the emotional winds her domestic trials were borne far and wide so that she sang as she drove homeward,

'Jurden water, black an' col'
Chills de body, not de soul
An' Ah wantah cross Jurden in uh calm time.'

She came from the barn to the kitchen door and stopped.

'Whut's de mattah, ol' satan, you ain't kickin' up yo' racket?' She addressed the snake's box. Complete silence. She went on into the house with a new hope in its birth struggles. Perhaps her threat to go to the white folks had frightened Sykes! Perhaps he was sorry! Fifteen years of misery and suppression had brought Delia to the place where she would hope *anything* that looked towards a way over or through her wall of inhibitions.

She felt in the match safe behind the stove at once for a match. There was only one there.

'Dat niggah wouldn't fetch nothing' heah tuh save his rotten neck, but he kin run thew whut Ah brings quick enough. Now he done toted off nigh on tuh haff uh box uh matches. He done had dat 'oman heah in mah house, too.'

Nobody but a woman could tell how she knew this even before she struck the match. But she did and it put her into a new fury.

Presently she brought in the tubs to put the white things to soak. This time she decided she need not bring the hamper out of the bedroom; she would go in there and do the sorting. She picked up the pot-bellied lamp and went in. The room was small and the hamper stood hard by the foot of the white iron bed. She could sit and reach through the bedposts – resting as she worked.

'Ah wantah cross Jurden in uh calm time.' She was singing again. The mood of the 'love feast' had returned. She threw back the lid of the basket almost gaily. Then, moved by both horror and terror, she sprang back towards the door. *There lay the snake in the basket!* He moved sluggishly at first, but even as she turned round and round, jumped up and down in an insanity of fear, he began to stir vigorously. She saw him pouring his awful beauty from the basket upon the bed, then she seized the lamp and ran as fast as she could to the kitchen. The wind from the open door blew out the light and the darkness added to her terror. She sped to the darkness of the yard, slamming the door after her before she thought to set down the lamp. She did not feel safe even on the ground, so she climed up in the hay barn.

There for an hour or more she lay sprawled upon the hay a gibbering wreck.

Finally she grew quiet, and after that, coherent thought. With this, stalked through her a cold, bloody rage. Hours of this. A period of introspection, a space of retrospection, then a mixture of both. Out of this an awful calm.

'Well, Ah done de bes' Ah could. If things ain't right, Gawd knows tain't mah fault.'

She went to sleep – a twitch sleep – and woke up to a faint gray sky. There was a loud hollow sound below. She peered out. Sykes was at the wood-pile, demolishing a wire-covered box.

He hurried to the kitchen door, but hung outside there some minutes before he entered, and stood some minutes more inside before he closed it after him.

The gray in the sky was spreading. Delia descended without fear now, and crouched beneath the low bedroom window. The drawn shade shut out the dawn, shut in the night. But the thin walls held back no sound.

'Dat ol' scratch is woke up now!' She mused at the tremendous whirr inside, which every woodsman knows, is one of the sound illusions. The rattle is a ventriloquist. His whirr sounds to the right, to the left, straight ahead, behind, close under foot – everywhere but where it is. Woe to him who guesses wrong unless he is prepared to hold up his end of the argument! Sometimes he strikes without rattling at all.

Inside, Sykes heard nothing until he knocked a pot lid off the stove while trying to reach the match safe in the dark. He had emptied his pockets at Bertha's.

The snake seemed to wake up under the stove and Sykes made a quick leap into the bedroom. In spite of the gin he had had, his head was clearning now.

'Mah Gawd!' he chattered, 'ef Ah could on'l strack uh light!'

The rattling ceased for a moment as he stood paralyzed. He waited. It seemed that the snake waited also.

'Oh, fuh de light! Ah thought he'd be too sick' – Sykes was muttering to himself when the whirr began again, close, right underfoot this time. Long before this, Sykes' ability to think had been flattened down to primitive instinct and he leapt – onto the bed.

Outside Delia heard a cry that might have come from a maddened chimpanzee, a stricken gorilla. All the terror, all the horror, all the rage that man possibly could express, without a recognizable human sound.

A tremendous stir inside there, another series of animal screams, the intermittent whirr of the reptile. The shade torn violently down from the window, letting in the red dawn, a huge brown hand seizing the window stick, great dull blows upon the wooden floor punctuating the gibberish of sound long after the rattle of the snake had abruptly subsided. All this Delia could see and hear from her place beneath the window, and it made her ill. She crept over to the four-o'clocks and stretched herself on the cool earth to recover.

She lay there. 'Delia, Delia!' She could hear Sykes calling in a most despairing tone as one who expected no answer. The sun crept on up, and he called. Delia could not move – her legs were gone flabby. She never moved, he called, and the sun kept rising.

'Mah Gawd!' She heard him moan, 'Mah Gawd fum Heben!' She heard him stumbling about and got up from her flower-bed. The sun was growing warm. As she approached the door she heard him call out hopefully, 'Delia, is dat you Ah heah?'

She saw him on his hands and knees as soon as she reached the door. He crept an inch or two toward her – all that he was able, and she saw his horribly swollen neck and this one open eye shining with hope. A surge of pity too strong to support bore her away from that eye that must, could not, fail to see the tubs. He would see the lamp. Orlando with its doctors was too far. She could scarcely reach the Chinaberry tree, where she waited in the growing heat while inside she knew the cold river was creeping up and up to extinguish that eye which must know by now that she knew.

The Conversion of the Jews

Philip Roth

'You're a real one for opening your mouth in the first place,' Itzie said. 'What do you open your mouth all the time for?'

'I didn't bring it up Itz, I didn't,' Ozzie said.

'What do you care about Jesus Christ for anyway?'

'I didn't bring up Jesus Christ. He did. I didn't even know what he was talking about. Jesus is historical, he kept saying. Jesus is historical.' Ozzie mimicked the monumental voice of Rabbi Binder.

'Jesus was a person that lived like you and me,' Ozzie continued. 'That's what Binder said—'

'Yeah?... So what! What do I give two cents whether he lived or not. And what do you gotta open your mouth!' Itzie Lieberman favored closed-mouthedness, especially when it came to Ozzie Freedman's questions. Mrs Freedman had to see Rabbi Binder twice before about Ozzie's questions and this Wednesday at four-thirty would be the third time. Itzie preferred to keep *his* mother in the kitchen; he settled for behind-the-back subtleties such as gestures, faces, snarls and other less delicate barnyard noises.

'He was a real person, Jesus, but he wasn't like God, and we don't believe he is God.' Slowly, Ozzie was explaining Rabbi Binder's position to Itzie, who had been absent from Hebrew School the previous afternoon.

'The Catholics,' Itzie said helpfully, 'they believe in Jesus Christ, that he's God.' Itzie Lieberman used 'the Catholics' in its broadest sense – to include the Protestants.

Ozzie received Itzie's remark with a tiny head bob, as though it were a footnote, and went on. 'His mother was Mary, and his father probably was Joseph,' Ozzie said. 'But the New Testament says his real father was God.'

'His *real* father?'

41

'Yeah,' Ozzie said, 'that's the big thing, his father's supposed to be God.'

'Bull.'

'That's what Rabbi Binder says, that it's impossible—'

'Sure it's impossible. That stuff's all bull. To have a baby you gotta get laid,' Itzie theologized. 'Mary hadda get laid.'

'That's what Binder says: "The only way a woman can have a baby is to have intercourse with a man."'

'He said *that*, Ozz?' For a moment it appeared that Itzie had put the theological question aside. 'He said that, intercourse?' A little curled smile shaped itself in the lower half of Itzie's face like a pink mustache. 'What you guys do, Ozz, you laugh or something?'

'I raised my hand.'

'Yeah? Whatja say?'

'That's when I asked the question.'

Itzie's face lit up. 'Whatja ask about – intercourse?'

'No, I asked the question about God, how if He could create the heaven and earth in six days, and make all the animals and the fish and the light in six days – the light especially, that's what always gets me, that He could make the light. Making fish and animals, that's pretty good—'

'That's damn good.' Itzie's appreciation was honest but unimaginative: it was as though God had just pitched a one-hitter.

'But making light... I mean when you think about it, it's really something,' Ozzie said. 'Anyway, I asked Binder if He could make all that in six days, and He could *pick* the six days he wanted right out of nowhere, why couldn't He let a woman have a baby without having intercourse.'

'You said intercourse, Ozz, to Binder?'

'Yeah.'

'Right in class?'

'Yeah.'

Itzie smacked the side of his head.

'I mean, no kidding around,' Ozzie said, 'that'd really be nothing. After all that other stuff, that'd practically be nothing.'

Itzie considered a moment. 'What'd Binder say?'

'He started all over again explaining how Jesus was historical and how he lived like you and me but he wasn't God. So I said I understood that. What I wanted to know was different.'

What Ozzie wanted to know was always different. The first time he had wanted to know how Rabbi Binder could call the Jews 'The Chosen People' if the Declaration of Independence claimed all men to be created equal. Rabbi Binder tried to distinguish for him between political equality and spiritual legitimacy, but what Ozzie wanted to know, he insisted vehemently, was different. That was the first time his mother had to come.

Then there was the plane crash. Fifty-eight people had been killed in a plane crash at La Guardia. In studying a casualty list in the newspaper his mother had discovered among the list of those dead eight Jewish names (his grandmother had nine but she counted Miller as a Jewish name): because of the eight she said the plane crash was 'a tragedy.' During free-discussion time on Wednesday Ozzie had brought to Rabbi Binder's attention this matter of 'some of his relations' always picking out the Jewish names. Rabbi Binder had begun to explain cultural unity and some other things when Ozzie stood up at his seat and said that what he wanted to know was different. Rabbi Binder insisted that he sit down and it was then that Ozzie shouted that he wished all fifty-eight were Jews. That was the second time his mother came.

'And he kept explaining about Jesus being historical, and so I kept asking him. No kidding, Itz, he was trying to make me look stupid.'

'So what he finally do?'

'Finally he starts screaming that I was deliberately simple-minded and a wise guy, and that my mother had to come, and this was the last time. And that I'd never get bar-mitzvahed if he could help it. Then, Itz, then he starts talking in that voice like a statue, real slow and deep, and he says that I better think over what I said about the Lord. He told me to go to his office and think it over.' Ozzie leaned his body towards Itzie. 'Itz, I thought it over for a solid hour, and now I'm convinced God could do it.'

Ozzie had planned to confess his latest transgression to his mother as soon as she came home from work. But it was a Friday night in November and already dark, and when Mrs Freedman came through the door she tossed off her coat, kissed Ozzie quickly on the face, and went to the kitchen table to light the three yellow candles, two for the Sabbath and one for Ozzie's father.

When his mother lit the candles she would move her two arms slowly towards her, dragging them through the air, as though persuading people whose minds were half made up. And her eyes would get glassy with tears. Even when his father was alive Ozzie remembered that her eyes had gotten glassy, so it didn't have anything to do with his dying. It had something to do with lighting the candles.

As she touched the flaming match to the unlit wick of a Sabbath candle, the phone rang, and Ozzie, standing only a foot from it, plucked it off the receiver and held it muffled to his chest. When his mother lit candles Ozzie felt there should be no noise: even breathing, if you could manage it, should be softened. Ozzie pressed the phone to his breast and watched his mother dragging whatever she was dragging, and he felt his own eyes get glassy. His mother was a round, tired, gray-haired penguin of a woman whose gray skin had begun to feel the tug of gravity and the weight of her own history. Even when she was dressed up she didn't look like a chosen person. But when she lit candles she looked like something better, like a woman who knew momentarily that God could do anything.

After a few mysterious minutes she was finished. Ozzie hung up the phone and walked to the kitchen table where she was beginning to lay the two places for the four-course Sabbath meal. He told her that she would have to see Rabbi Binder next Wednesday at four-thirty, and then he told her why. For the first time in their life together she hit Ozzie across the face with her hand.

All through the chopped liver and chicken soup part of the dinner Ozzie cried; he didn't have any appetite for the rest.

On Wednesday, in the largest of the three basement classrooms of the synagogue, Rabbi Marvin Binder, a tall, handsome, broad-shouldered man of thirty with thick strong-fibered black hair, removed his watch from his pocket and saw that it was four o'clock. At the rear of the room Yakov Blotnik, the seventy-one-year-old custodian, slowly polished the large window, mumbling to himself, unaware that it was four o'clock or six o'clock, Monday or Wednesday. To most of the students Yakov Blotnik's mumbling, along with his brown curly beard, scythe nose, and two heel-trailing black cats, made of him an object of wonder, a foreigner, a relic, towards whom they were alternately fearful and disrespectful. To Ozzie the mumbling had always seemed a monotonous, curious prayer; what made it curious was that old Blotnik had been mumbling so steadily for so many years, Ozzie suspected he had memorized the prayers and forgotten all about God.

'It is now free-discussion time,' Rabbi Binder said. 'Feel free to talk about any Jewish matter at all – religion, family, politics, sports—'

There was silence. It was a gusty, clouded November afternoon and it did not seem as though there ever was or could be a thing called baseball. So nobody this week said a word about that hero from the past, Hank Greenberg – which limited free discussion considerably.

And the soul-battering Ozzie Freedman had just received from Rabbi Binder had imposed its limitation. When it was Ozzie's turn to read aloud from the Hebrew book the rabbi had asked him petulantly why he didn't read more rapidly. He was showing no progress. Ozzie said he could read faster but that if he did he was sure not to understand what he was reading. Nevertheless, at the rabbi's repeated suggestion Ozzie tried, and showed a great talent, but in the midst of a long passage he stopped short and said he didn't understand a word he was reading, and started in again at a drag-footed pace. Then came the soul-battering.

Consequently when free-discussion time rolled around none of the students felt too free. The rabbi's invitation was answered only by the mumblings of feeble old Blotnik.

'Isn't there anything at all you would like to discuss?' Rabbi Binder asked again, looking at his watch. 'No questions or comments?'

There was a small grumble from the third row. The rabbi requested that Ozzie rise and give the rest of the class the advantage of his thought.

Ozzie rose. 'I forget it now,' he said, and sat down in his place.

Rabbi Binder advanced a seat towards Ozzie and poised himself on the edge of the desk. It was Itzie's desk and the rabbi's frame only a dagger's length away from his face snapped him to sitting attention.

'Stand up again, Oscar,' Rabbi Binder said calmly, 'and try to assemble your thoughts.'

Ozzie stood up. All his classmates turned in their seats and watched as he gave an unconvincing scratch to his forehead.

'I can't assemble any,' he announced, and plunked himself down.

'Stand up!' Rabbi Binder advanced from Itzie's desk to the one directly in front of Ozzie; when the rabbinical back was turned Itzie gave it five-fingers off the top of his nose, causing a small titter in the room. Rabbi Binder was too absorbed in squelching Ozzie's nonsense once and for all to bother with titters. 'Stand up, Oscar. What's your question about?'

Ozzie pulled a word out of the air. It was the handiest word. 'Religion.'

'Oh, now you remember?'

'Yes.'

'What is it?'

Trapped, Ozzie blurted the first thing that came to him. 'Why can't He make anything He wants to make!'

As Rabbi Binder prepared an answer, a final answer, Itzie, ten feet behind him, raised one finger on his left hand, gestured it meaningfully towards the rabbi's back, and brought the house down.

Binder twisted quickly to see what had happened and in the midst of the commotion Ozzie shouted into the rabbi's back what he couldn't have shouted to his face. It was a loud, toneless sound that had the timbre of something stored inside for about six days.

'You don't know! You don't know anything about God!'

The rabbi spun back towards Ozzie. 'What?'

'You don't know – you don't—'

'Apologize, Oscar, apologize!' It was a threat.

'You don't—'

Rabbi Binder's hand flicked out at Ozzie's cheek. Perhaps it had only been meant to clamp the boy's mouth shut, but Ozzie ducked and the palm caught him squarely on the nose.

The blood came in a short, red spurt on to Ozzie's shirt front.

The next moment was all confusion. Ozzie screamed, 'You b.....d, you b.....d!' and broke for the classroom door. Rabbi Binder lurched a step backwards, as though his own blood had started flowing violently in the opposite direction, then gave a clumsy lurch forward and bolted out the door after Ozzie. The class followed after the rabbi's huge blue-suited back, and before old Blotnik could turn from his window, the room was empty and everyone was headed full speed up the three flights leading to the roof.

If one should compare the light of day to the life of man: sunrise to birth; sunset – the dropping down over the edge – to death; then as Ozzie Freedman wiggled through the trapdoor of the synagogue roof, his feet kicking backwards bronco-style at Rabbi Binder's outstretched arms – at that moment the day was fifty years old. As a rule, fifty or fifty-five reflects accurately the age of late afternoons in November, for it is in that month, during those hours, that one's awareness of light seems no longer a matter of seeing, but of hearing: light begins clicking away. In fact, as Ozzie locked shut the trapdoor in the rabbi's face, the sharp click of the bolt into the lock might momentarily have been mistaken for the sound of the heavier gray that had just throbbed through the sky.

With all his weight Ozzie kneeled on the locked door; any instant he was certain that Rabbi Binder's shoulder would fling it open, splintering the wood into shrapnel and catapulting his body into the sky. But the door did not move and below him he heard only the rumble of feet, first loud then dim, like thunder rolling away.

A question shot through his brain. 'Can this be *me*?' For a thirteen-year-old who had just labeled his religious leader a b.....d, twice, it was not an improper question. Louder and louder the question came to him – 'Is it me? Is it me?' – until he discovered himself no longer kneeling, but racing crazily towards the edge of the roof, his eyes crying, his throat screaming, and his arms flying every which way as though not his own.

'Is it me? Is it me Me ME ME ME! It has to be me – but is it!'

It is the question a thief must ask himself the night he jimmies open his first window, and it is said to be the question with which bridegrooms quiz themselves before the altar.

In the few wild seconds it took Ozzie's body to propel him to the edge of the roof, his self-examination began to grow fuzzy. Gazing down at the street, he became confused as to the problem beneath the question: was it, is-it-me-who-called-Binder-a-b.....d? or, is-it-me-prancing-around-on-the-roof? How ever, the scene below settled all, for there is an instant in any action when whether it is you or somebody else is academic. The thief crams the money in his pockets and scoots out the window. The bridegroom signs the hotel register for two. And the boy on the roof finds a streetful of people gaping at him, necks stretched backwards, faces up, as though he were the ceiling of the Hayden Planetarium. Suddenly you know it's you.

'Oscar! Oscar Freedman!' A voice rose from the center of the crowd, a voice that, could it have been seen, would have looked like the writing on scroll. 'Oscar Freedman, get down from there. Immediately!' Rabbi Binder was pointing one arm stiffly up at him; and at the end of that arm, one finger aimed menacingly. It was the attitude of a dictator, but one – the eyes confessed all – whose personal valet had spit neatly in his face.

Ozzie didn't answer. Only for a blink's length did he look towards Rabbi Binder. Instead his eyes began to fit together the world beneath him, to sort out people from places, friends from enemies, participants from spectators. In little jagged starlike clusters his friends stood around Rabbi Binder, who was still pointing. The topmost point on a star compounded not of angles but of five adolescent boys was Itzie. What a world it was, with those stars below, Rabbi Binder below... Ozzie, who a moment earlier hadn't been able to control his own body, started to feel the meaning of the word control: he felt Peace and he felt Power.

'Oscar Freedman, I'll give you three to come down.'

Few dictators give their subjects three to do anything; but, as always, Rabbi Binder only looked dictatorial.

'Are you ready, Oscar?'

Ozzie nodded his head yes, although he had no intention in the world – the lower one or the celestial one he'd just entered – of coming down even if Rabbi Binder should give him a million.

'All right then,' said Rabbi Binder. He ran a hand through his black Samson hair as though it were the gesture prescribed for uttering the first digit. Then, with his other hand cutting a circle out of the small piece of sky around him, he spoke. 'One!'

There was no thunder. On the contrary, at that moment, as though 'one' was the cue for which he had been waiting, the world's least thunderous person appeared on the synagogue steps. He did not so much come out of the synagogue door as lean out, onto the darkening air. He clutched at the doorknob with one hand and looked up at the roof.

'Oy!'

Yakov Blotnik's old mind hobbled slowly, as if on crutches, and though he couldn't decide precisely what the boy was doing on the roof, he knew it wasn't good – that is, it wasn't-good-for-the-Jews. For Yakov Blotnik life had fractionated itself simply: things were either good-for-the-Jews or no-good for-the-Jews.

He smacked his free hand to his in-sucked cheeks, gently. 'Oy, Gut!' And, then quickly as he was able, he jacked down his head and surveyed the street. There was Rabbi Binder (like a man at an auction with only three dollars in his pocket, he had just delivered a shaky 'Two!'); there were the students, and that was all. So far it wasn't-so-bad-for-the-Jews. But the boy had to come down immediately, before anybody saw. The problem: how to get the boy off the roof?

Anybody who has ever had a cat on the roof knows how to get him down. You call the fire department. Or first you call the operator and you ask her for the fire department. And the next thing there is great jamming of brakes and clanging of bells and shouting of instructions. And then the cat is off the roof. You do the same thing to get a boy off the roof.

That is, you do the same thing if you are Yakov Blotnik and you once had a cat on the roof.

When the engines, all four of them, arrived, Rabbi Binder had four times given Ozzie the count of three. The big hook-and-ladder swung around the corner and one of the firemen leaped from it, plunging headlong towards the yellow fire hydrant in front of the synagogue. With a huge wrench he began to unscrew the top nozzle. Rabbi Binder raced over to him and pulled at his shoulder.

'There's no fire...'

The fireman mumbled back over his shoulder and, heatedly, continued working at the nozzle.

'But there's no fire, there's no fire...' Binder shouted. When the fireman mumbled again, the rabbi grasped his face with both his hands and pointed it up at the roof.

To Ozzie it looked as though Rabbi Binder was trying to tug the fireman's head out of his body, like a cork from a bottle. He had to giggle at the picture they made; it was a family portrait – rabbi in black skullcap, fireman in red fire hat, and the little yellow hydrant squatting beside like a kid brother, bareheaded. From the edge of the roof Ozzie waved at the portrait, a one-handed, flapping, mocking wave: in doing it his right foot slipped from under him. Rabbi Binder covered his eyes with his hands.

Firemen work fast. Before Ozzie had even regained his balance, a big, round, yellowed net was being held on the synagogue lawn. The firemen who held it looked up at Ozzie with stern, feelingless faces.

One of the firemen turned his head towards Rabbi Binder. 'What, is the kid nuts or something?'

Rabbi Binder unpeeled his hands from his eyes, slowly, painfully, as if they were tape. Then he checked: nothing on the sidewalk, no dents in the net.

'Is he gonna jump, or what?' the fireman shouted.

In a voice not at all like a statue, Rabbi Binder finally answered. 'Yes, Yes, I think so... He's been threatening to...'

Threatening to? Why, the reason he was on the roof, Ozzie remembered, was to get away; he hadn't even thought about jumping. He had just run to get away, and the truth was that he hadn't really headed for the roof as much as he'd been chased there.

'What's his name, the kid?'

'Freedman,' Rabbi Binder answered. 'Oscar Freedman.'

The fireman looked up at Ozzie. 'What is it with you, Oscar? You gonna jump, or what?'

Ozzie did not answer. Frankly, the question had just arisen.

'Look, Oscar, if you're gonna jump, jump – and if you're not gonna jump, don't jump. But don't waste our time, will ya?'

Ozzie looked at the fireman and then at Rabbi Binder. He wanted to see Rabbi Binder cover his eyes one more time.

'I'm going to jump.'

And then he scampered around the edge of the roof to the corner, where there was no net below, and he flapped his arms at his sides, swishing the air and smacking his palms to his trousers on the downbeat. He began screaming like some kind of engine. 'Wheeeee... wheeeeee,' and leaning way out over the edge with the upper half of his body. The fireman whipped around to cover the ground with the net. Rabbi Binder mumbled a few words to Somebody and covered his eyes. Everything happened quickly, jerkily, as in a silent movie. The crowd, which had arrived with the fire engines, gave out a long, Fourth-of-July fireworks oooh-aahhh. In the excitement no one had paid the crowd much heed, except, of course, Yakov Blotnik, who swung from the doorknob counting heads. 'Fier und tsvansik... finf und tsvantsik... Oy, Gut!' It wasn't like this with the cat.

Rabbi Binder peeked through his fingers, checked the sidewalk and net. Empty. But there was Ozzie racing to the other corner. The firemen raced with him but were unable to keep up. Whenever Ozzie wanted to he might jump and splatter himself upon the sidewalk and by the time the firemen scooted to the spot all they could do with their net would be to cover the mess.

'Wheeeee... wheeeee...'

'Hey, Oscar,' the winded fireman yelled, 'What the hell is this, a game or something?'

'Wheeeee... wheeeee...'

'Hey, Oscar—'

But he was off now to the other corner, flapping his wings fiercely. Rabbi Binder couldn't take it any longer – the fire engines from nowhere, the screaming suicidal boy, the net. He fell to his knees, exhausted, and with his hands curled together in front of his chest like a little dome, he pleaded, 'Oscar, stop it, Oscar. Don't jump, Oscar. Please come down... Please don't jump.'

And further back in the crowd a single voice, a single young voice, shouted a lone word to the boy on the roof.

'Jump!'

It was Itzie. Ozzie momentarily stopped flapping.

'Go ahead, Ozz – jump! Itzie broke off his point of the star and courageously, with the inspiration not of a wise-guy but of a disciple, stood alone. 'Jump, Ozz, jump!'

Still on his knees, his hands still curled, Rabbi Binder twisted his body back. He looked at Itzie, then, agonizingly, back to Ozzie.

'OSCAR, DON'T JUMP! PLEASE, DON'T JUMP... please, please...'

'Jump!' This time it wasn't Itzie but another point of the star. By the time Mrs Freedman arrived to keep her four-thirty appointment with Rabbi Binder, the whole little upside down heaven was shouting and pleading for Ozzie to jump, and Rabbi Binder no longer was pleading with him not to jump, but was crying into the dome of his hands.

Understandably Mrs Freedman couldn't figure out what her son was doing on the roof. So she asked.

'Ozzie, my Ozzie, what are you doing? My Ozzie, what is it?'

Ozzie stopped wheeeeeing and slowed his arms down to a cruising flap, the kind birds use in soft winds, but he did not answer. He stood against the low, clouded, darkening sky – light clicked down swiftly now, as on a small gear – flapping softly and gazing down at the small bundle of a woman who was his mother.

'What are you doing, Ozzie?' She turned towards the kneeling Rabbi Binder and rushed so close that only a paper-thickness of dusk lay between her stomach and his shoulders.

'What is my baby doing?'

Rabbi Binder gaped up at her but he too was mute. All that moved was the dome of his hands; it shook back and forth like a weak pulse.

'Rabbi, get him down! He'll kill himself. Get him down, my only baby...'

'I can't,' Rabbi Binder said, 'I can't...' and he turned his handsome head towards the crowd of boys behind him. 'It's them. Listen to them.'

And for the first time Mrs Freedman saw the crowd of boys, and she heard what they were yelling.

'He's doing it for them. He won't listen to me. It's them.' Rabbi Binder spoke like one in a trance.

'For them?'

'Yes.'

'Why for them?'

'They want him to...'

Mrs Freedman raised her two arms upward as though she were conducting the sky. 'For them he's doing it!' And then in a gesture older than pyramids, older than prophets and floods, her arms came slapping down to her sides. 'A martyr I have. Look!' She tilted her head to the roof. Ozzie was still flapping softly. 'My martyr.'

'Oscar, come down, *please*,' Rabbi Binder groaned.

In a startlingly even voice Mrs Freedman called to the boy on the roof. 'Ozzie, come down, Ozzie. Don't be a martyr, my baby.'

As though it were a litany, Rabbi Binder repeated her words. 'Don't be a martyr, my baby. Don't be a martyr.'

'Gawhead, Ozz – *be* a Martin!' It was Itzie. 'Be a Martin, be a Martin,' and all the voices joined in singing for Martindom, what ever *it* was. 'Be a Martin, be a Martin...'

Somehow when you're on a roof the darker it gets the less you can hear. All Ozzie knew was that two groups wanted two new things: his friends were spirited and musical about what they wanted; his mother and the rabbi were even-toned, chanting, about what they didn't want. The rabbi's voice was without tears now and so was his mother's.

The big net stared up at Ozzie like a sightless eye. The big, clouded sky pushed down. From beneath it looked like a gray corrugated board. Suddenly, looking up into that unsympathetic sky, Ozzie realized all the strangeness of what these people, his friends, were asking: they wanted him to jump, to kill himself; they were singing about it now – it made them that happy. And there was an even greater strangeness: Rabbi Binder was on his knees, trembling. If there was a question to be asked now it was not 'Is it me?' but rather 'Is it us... Is it us?'

Being on the roof, it turned out, was a serious thing. If he jumped would the singing become dancing? Would it? What would jumping stop? Yearningly, Ozzie wished he could rip open the sky, plunge his hands through, and pull out the sun; and on the sun, like a coin, would be stamped JUMP or DON'T JUMP.

Ozzie's knees rocked and sagged a little under him as though they were setting him for a dive. His arms tightened, stiffened, froze, from shoulders to fingernails. He felt as if each part of his body were going to vote as to whether he should kill himself or not – and each part as though it were independent of *him*.

The light took an unexpected click down and the new darkness, like a gag, hushed the friends singing for this and the mother and rabbi chanting for that.

Ozzie stopped counting votes, and in a curiously high voice, like one who wasn't prepared for speech, he spoke.

'Mamma?'

'Yes, Oscar.'

'Mamma, get down on your knees, like Rabbi Binder.'

'Oscar—'

'Get down on your knees,' he said, 'or I'll jump.'

Ozzie heard a whimper, then a quick rustling, and when he looked down where his mother had stood he saw the top of a head and beneath that a circle of dress. She was kneeling beside Rabbi Binder.

He spoke again. 'Everybody kneel.' There was the sound of everybody kneeling.

Ozzie looked around. With one hand he pointed towards the synagogue entrance. 'Make *him* kneel.'

There was a noise, not of kneeling, but of body-and-cloth stretching. Ozzie could hear Rabbi Binder saying in a gruff whisper, '...or he'll *kill* himself,' and when next he looked there was Yakov Blotnik off the doorknob and for the first time in his life upon his knees in the Gentile posture of prayer.

As for the firemen – it is not as difficult as one might imagine to hold a net taut while you are kneeling.

Ozzie looked around again; and then he called to Rabbi Binder.

'Rabbi?'

'Yes, Oscar.'

'Rabbi Binder, do you believe in God?'

'Yes.'

'Do you believe God can do Anything?' Ozzie leaned his head out into the darkness. 'Anything?'

'Oscar, I think—'

'Tell me you believe God can do Anything.'

There was a second's hesitation. Then: 'God can do Anything.'

'Tell me you believe God can make a child without intercourse.'

'He can.'

'Tell me!'

'God,' Rabbi Binder admitted, 'can make a child without intercourse.'

'Mamma, you tell me.'

'God can make a child without intercourse,' his mother said.

'Make him tell me.' There was no doubt who *him* was.

In a few moments Ozzie heard an old comical voice say something to the increasing darkness about God.

Next, Ozzie made everybody say it. And then he made them all say they believed in Jesus Christ – first one at a time, then all together.

When the catechizing was through it was the beginning of evening. From the street it sounded as if the boy on the roof might have sighed.

'Ozzie?' A woman's voice dared to speak. 'You'll come down now?'

There as no answer, but the woman waited, and when a voice finally did speak it was thin and crying, and exhausted as that of an old man who had just finished pulling the bells.

'Mamma, don't you see – you shouldn't hit me. He shouldn't hit me. You shouldn't hit me about God, Mamma. You should never hit anybody about God—'

'Ozzie, please come down now.'

'Promise me, promise me you'll never hit anybody about God.'

He had asked only his mother, but for some reason everyone kneeling in the street promised he would never hit anybody about God.

Once again there was silence.

'I can come down now, Mamma,' the boy on the roof finally said. He turned his head both ways as though checking the traffic lights. 'Now I can come down...'

And he did, right into the center of the yellow net that glowed in the evening's edge like a overgrown halo.

Dry September

William Faulkner

I

Through the bloody September twilight, aftermath of sixty-two rainless days, it had gone like a fire in dry grass – the rumor, the story, whatever it was. Something about Miss Minnie Cooper and a Negro. Attacked, insulted, frightened: none of them, gathered in the barber shop on that Saturday evening where the ceiling fan stirred, without freshening it, the vitiated air, sending back upon them, in recurrent surges of stale pomade and lotion, their own stale breath and odors, knew exactly what had happened.

'Except it wasn't Will Mayes,' a barber said. He was a man of middle age; a thin, sand-colored man with a mild face, who was shaving a client.

'I know Will Mayes. He's a good nigger. And I know Miss Minnie Cooper, too.'

'What do you know about her?' a second barber said.

'Who is she?' the client said. 'A young girl?'

'No,' the barber said. 'She's about forty, I reckon. She ain't married. That's why I don't believe—'

'Believe, hell!' a hulking youth in a sweat-stained silk shirt said. 'Won't you take a white woman's word before a nigger's?'

'I don't believe Will Mayes did it,' the barber said. 'I know Will Mayes.'

'Maybe you know who did it, then. Maybe you already got him out of town, you damn niggerlover.'

'I don't believe anybody did anything. I don't believe anything happened. I leave it to you fellows if them ladies that get old without getting married don't have notions that a man can't—'

'Then you are a hell of a white man,' the client said. He moved under the cloth. The youth had sprung to his feet.

'You don't?' he said. 'Do you accuse a white woman of lying?'

The barber held the razor poised above the half-risen client. He did not look around.

'It's this durn weather,' another said. 'It's enough to make a man do anything. Even to her.'

Nobody laughed. The barber said in his mild, stubborn tone: 'I ain't accusing nobody of nothing. I just know and you fellows know how a woman that never—'

'You damn niggerlover!' the youth said.

'Shut up, Butch,' another said. 'We'll get the facts in plenty of time to act.'

'Who is? Who's getting them?' the youth said. 'Facts, hell! I—'

'You're a fine white man,' the client said. 'Ain't you?' In his frothy beard he looked like a desert rat in the moving pictures. 'You tell them, Jack,' he said to the youth. 'If there ain't any white men in this town, you can count on me, even if I ain't only a drummer and a stranger.'

'That's right, boys,' the barber said. 'Find out the truth first. I know Will Mayes.'

'Well, by God!' the youth shouted. 'To think that a white man in this town—'

'Shut up, Butch,' the second speaker said. 'We got plenty of time.'

The client sat up. He looked at the speaker. 'Do you claim that anything excuses a nigger attacking a white woman? Do you mean to tell me you are a white man and you'll stand for it? You better go back North where you came from. The South don't want your kind here.'

'North what?' the second said. 'I was born and raised in this town.'

'Well, by God!' the youth said. He looked about with a strained, baffled gaze, as if he was trying to remember what it was he wanted to say or to do. He drew his sleeve across his sweating face. 'Damn if I'm going to let a white woman—'

'You tell them, Jack,' the drummer said. 'By God, if they—'

The screen door crashed open. A man stood in the floor, his feet apart and his heavy-set body poised easily. His white shirt was open at the throat; he wore a felt hat. His hot, bold glance swept the group. His name was McLendon. He had commanded troops at the front in France and had been decorated for valor.

'Well,' he said, 'are you going to sit there and let a black son rape a white woman on the streets of Jefferson?'

Butch sprang up again. The silk of his shirt clung flat to his heavy shoulders. At each armpit was a dark halfmoon. 'That's what I been telling them! That's what I—'

'Did it really happen?' a third said. 'This ain't the first man scare she ever had, like Hawkshaw says. What's that?' The barber had been slowly forcing him back into the chair; he arrested himself reclining, his head lifted, the barber still pressing him down.

McLendon whirled on the third speaker. 'Happen? What the hell difference does it make? Are you going to let the black sons get away with it until one really does it?'

'That's what I'm telling them!' Butch shouted. He cursed, long and steady, pointless.

'Here, here,' a fourth said. 'Not so loud. Don't talk so loud.'

'Sure,' McLendon said; 'no talking necessary at all. I've done my talking. Who's with me?' He poised on the balls of his feet, roving his gaze.

The barber held the drummer's face down, the razor poised. 'Find out the facts first, boys. I know Willy Mayes. It wasn't him. Let's get the sheriff and do this thing right.'

McLendon whirled upon him his furious, rigid face. The barber did not look away. They looked like men of different races. The other barbers had ceased also above their prone clients. 'You mean to tell me,' McLendon said, 'that you'd take a nigger's word before a white woman's? Why, you damn niggerloving—'

The third speaker rose and grasped McLendon's arm; he too had been a soldier. 'Now, now. Let's figure this thing out. Who knows anything about what really happened?'

'Figure out hell!' McLendon jerked his arm free. 'All that're with me get up from there. The ones that ain't—' He roved his gaze, dragging his sleeve across his face.

Three men rose. The drummer in the chair sat up. 'Here,' he said, jerking at the cloth about his neck; 'get this rag off me. I'm with him. I don't live here, but by God, if our mothers and wives and sisters—' He smeared the cloth over his face and flung it to the floor. McLendon stood in the floor and cursed the others. Another rose and moved toward him. The remainder sat uncomfortable, not looking at one another, then one by one they rose and joined him.

The barber picked the cloth from the floor. He began to fold it neatly. 'Boys, don't do that. Will Mayes never done it. I know.'

'Come on,' McLendon said. He whirled. From his hip pocket protruded the butt of a heavy automatic pistol. They went out. The screen door crashed behind them reverberant in the dead air.

The barber wiped the razor carefully and swiftly, and put it away, and ran to the rear, and took his hat from the wall. 'I'll be back as soon as I can,' he said to the other barbers. 'I can't let—' He went out, running. The two other barbers followed him to the door and caught it on the rebound, leaning out and looking up the street after him. The air was flat and dead. It had a metallic taste at the base of the tongue.

'What can he do?' the first said. The second one was saying 'Jees Christ, Jees Christ' under his breath. 'I'd just as lief be Will Mayes as Hawk, if he gets McLendon riled.'

'Jees Christ, Jees Christ,' the second whisper.

'You reckon he really done it to her?' the first said.

II

She was thirty-eight or thirty-nine. She lived in a small frame house with her invalid mother and a thin, sallow, unflagging aunt, where each morning between ten and eleven she would appear on the porch in a lace-trimmed boudoir cap, to sit swinging in the porch swing until noon. After dinner she lay down for a while, until the afternoon began to cool. Then in one of the three or four new voile dresses which she had each summer, she would go downtown to spend the afternoon in the stores with the other ladies, where they would handle the goods and haggle over the prices in cold, immediate voices, without any intention of buying.

She was of comfortable people – not the best in Jefferson, but good people enough – and she was still on the slender side of ordinary looking, with a bright, faintly haggard manner and dress. When she was young she had had a slender, nervous body and a sort of hard vivacity which had enabled her for a time to ride upon the crest of the town's social life as exemplified by the high school party and church social period of her contemporaries while still children enough to be unclassconscious.

She was the last to realize that she was losing ground; that those among whom she had been a little brighter and louder flame than any other were beginning to learn the pleasure of snobbery – male – and retaliation – female. That was when her face began to wear that bright, haggard look. She still carried it to parties on the shadowy porticoes and summer lawns, like a mask or a flag, with that bafflement of furious repudiation of truth in he eyes. One evening at a party she heard a boy and two girls, all schoolmates, talking. She never accepted another invitation.

She watched the girls with whom she had grown up as they married and got homes and children, but no man ever called on her steadily until the children of the other girls had been calling her 'aunty' for several years, the while their mothers told them in bright voices about how popular Aunt Minnie had been as a girl. Then the town began to see her driving on Sunday afternoons with the cashier in the bank. He was a widower of about forty – a high-colored man, smelling always faintly of the barber shop or of whisky. He owned the first automobile in town, a red runabout; Minnie had the first motoring bonnet and veil the town ever saw. Then the town began to say: 'Poor Minnie.' 'But she is old enough to take care of herself,' others said. That was when she began to ask her old schoolmates that their children call her 'cousin' instead of 'aunty'.

It was twelve years now since she had been relegated into adultery by public opinion, and eight years since the cashier had gone to a Memphis bank, returning for one day each Christmas, which he spent at an annual bachelors' party at a hunting club on the river. From behind their curtains the neighbors would see the party pass, and during the over-the-way Christmas day visiting they would tell her about him, about how well he looked, and how they heard that he was prospering in the city, watching with bright, secret eyes her haggard, bright face. Usually by that hour there would be the scent of whisky on her breath. It was supplied her by a youth, a clerk at the soda fountain: 'Sure; I buy it for the old gal. I reckon she's entitled to a little fun.'

Her mother kept to her room altogether now; the gaunt aunt ran the house. Against that background Minnie's bright dresses, her idle and empty days, had a quality of furious unreality. She went out in the evenings only with women now, neighbors, to the moving pictures. Each afternoon she dressed in one of the new dresses and went downtown alone, where her young 'cousins' were already strolling in the late afternoons with their delicate, silken heads and thin, awkward arms and conscious hips, clinging to one another or shrieking and giggling with paired boys in the soda fountain when she passed and went on along the serried store fronts, in the doors of which the sitting and lounging men did not even follow her with their eyes any more.

III

The barber went swiftly up the street where the sparse lights, insect-swirled, glared in rigid and violent suspension in the lifeless air. The day had died in a pall of dust; above the darkened square, shrouded by the spent dust, the sky was as clear as the inside of a brass bell. Below the east was a rumor of the twice-waxed moon.

When he overtook them McLendon and three others were getting into a car parked in an alley. McLendon stooped his thick head, peering out beneath the top. 'Changed your mind, did you?' he said. 'Damn good thing; by God, tomorrow when this town hears about how you talked tonight—'

'Now, now,' the other ex-soldier said. 'Hawkshaw's all right. Come on, Hawk; jump in.'

'Will Mayes never done it, boys,' the barber said. 'If anybody done it. Why, you all know well as I do there ain't any town where they got better niggers than us. And you know how a lady will kind of think things about men when there sure ain't any reason to, and Miss Minnie anyway—'

'Sure, sure,' the soldier said. 'We're just going to talk to him a little that's all.'

'Talk hell!' Butch said. 'When we're through with the—'

'Shut up, for God's sake!' the soldier said. 'Do you want everybody in town—'

'Tell them, by God!' McLendon said. 'Tell every one of the sons that'll let a white woman—'

'Let's go; let's go: here's the other car.' The second car slid squealing out of a cloud of dust at the alley mouth. McLendon started his car and took the lead. Dust lay like fog in the street. The street lights hung nimbused as in water. They drove on out of town.

A rutted lane turned at right angles. Dust hung above it too, and above all the land. The dark bulk of the ice plant, where the Negro Mayes was night watchman, rose against the sky. 'Better stop here, hadn't we?' the soldier said. McLendon did not reply. He hurled the car up and slammed to a stop, the headlights glaring on the blank wall.

'Listen here, boys,' the barber said; 'if he's here, don't that prove he never done it? Don't it? If it was him, he would run. Don't you see he would?' The second car came up and stopped. McLendon got down; Butch sprang down beside him. 'Listen, boys,' the barber said.

'Cut the lights off!' McLendon said. The breathless dark rushed down. There was no sound in it save their lungs as they sought air in the parched dust in which for two months they had lived; then the diminishing crunch of McLendon's and Butch's feet, and a moment later McLendon's voice:

'Will!... Will!'

Below the east the wan hemorrhage of the moon increased. It heaved above the ridge, silvering the air, the dust, so that they seemed to breathe, live, in a bowl of molten lead. There was no sound of nightbird nor insect, no sound save their breathing and a faint ticking of contracting metal about the cars. Where their bodies touched one another they seemed to sweat dryly, for no more moisture came. 'Christ!' a voice said; 'let's get out of here.'

But they didn't move until vague noises began to grow out of the darkness ahead; then they got out and waited tensely in the breathless dark. There was another sound: a blow, a hissing expulsion of breath and McLendon cursing in undertone. They stood for a moment longer, then they ran forward. They ran in a stumbling clump, as though they were fleeing something. 'Kill him, kill the son,' a voice whispered. McLendon flung them back.

'Not here,' he said. 'Get him into the car.' 'Kill him, kill the black son!' the voice murmured. They dragged the Negro to the car. The barber had waited beside the car. He could feel himself sweating and he knew he was going to be sick at the stomach.

'What is it, captains?' the Negro said. 'I ain't done nothing. 'Fore God, Mr John.' Someone produced handcuffs. They worked busily about the Negro as though he were a post, quiet, intent, getting in one another's way. He submitted to the handcuffs, looking swiftly and constantly from dim face to dim face. 'Who's here, captains?' he said, leaning to peer into the faces until they could feel his breath and smell his sweaty reek. He spoke a name or two. 'What you all say I done, Mr John?'

McLendon jerked the car door open. 'Get in!' he said.

The Negro did not move. 'What you all going to do with me, Mr John? I ain't done nothing. White folks, captains, I ain't done nothing: I swear 'fore God.' He called another name.

'Get in!' McLendon said. He struck the Negro. The others expelled their breath in a dry hissing and struck him with random blows and he whirled and cursed them, and swept his manacled hands across their faces and slashed the barber upon the mouth, and the barber struck him also. 'Get him in there,' McLendon said. They pushed at him. He ceased struggling and got in and sat quietly as the others took their places. He sat between the barber and the soldier, drawing his limbs in so as not to touch them, his eyes going swiftly and constantly from face to face. Butch clung to the running board. The car moved on. The barber nursed his mouth with his handkerchief.

'What's the matter, Hawk?' the soldier said.

'Nothing,' the barber said. They regained the highroad and turned away from town. The second car dropped back out of the dust. They went on, gaining speed; the final fringe of houses dropped behind.

'Goddam, he stinks!' the soldier said.

'We'll fix that,' the drummer in front beside McLendon said. On the running board Butch cursed into the hot rush of air. The barber leaned suddenly forward and touched McLendon's arm.

'Let me out, John,' he said.

'Jump out, niggerlover,' McLendon said without turning his head. He drove swiftly. Behind them the sourceless lights of the second car glared in the dust. Presently McLendon turned into a narrow road. It was rutted with disuse. It led back to an abandoned brick kiln – a series of reddish mounds and weeds- and vine-choked vats without bottom. It had been used for pasture once, until one day the owner missed one of his mules. Although he prodded carefully in the vats with a long pole, he could not even find the bottom of them.

'John,' the barber said.

'Jump out, then,' McLendon said, hurling the car along the ruts. Beside the barber the Negro spoke:

'Mr Henry.'

The barber sat forward. The narrow tunnel of the road rushed up and past. Their motion was like an extinct furnace blast: cooler, but utterly dead. The car bounded from rut to rut.

'Mr Henry,' the Negro said.

The barber began to tug furiously at the door. 'Look out, there!' the soldier said, but the barber had already kicked the door open and swung onto the running board. The soldier leaned across the Negro and grasped at him, but he had already jumped. The car went on without checking speed.

The impetus hurled him crashing through dust-sheathed weeds, into the ditch. Dust puffed about him, and in a thin, vicious crackling of sapless stems he lay choking and retching until the second car passed and died away. Then he rose and limped on until he reached the highroad and turned toward town, brushing at his clothes with his hands. The moon was higher, riding high and clear of the dust at last, and after a while the town began to glare beneath the dust. He went on, limping. Presently he heard cars and the glow of them grew in the dust behind him and he left the road and crouched again in the weeds until they passed. McLendon's car came last now. There were four people in it and Butch was not on the running board.

They went on; the dust swallowed them; the glare and the sound died away. The dust of them hung for a while, but soon the eternal dust absorbed it again. The barber climbed back onto the road and limped on toward town.

IV

As she dressed for supper on that Saturday evening, her own flesh felt like fever. Her hands trembled among the hooks and eyes, and her eyes had a feverish look, and her hair swirled crisp and crackling under the comb. While she was still dressing the friends called for her and sat while she donned her sheerest underthings and stockings and a new voile dress. 'Do you feel strong enough to go out?' they said, their eyes bright too, with a dark glitter. 'When you have had time to get over the shock, you must tell us what happened. What he said and did; everything.'

In the leafed darkness, as they walked toward the square, she began to breathe deeply, something like a swimmer preparing to dive, until she ceased trembling, the four of them walking slowly because of the terrible heat and out of solicitude for her. But as they neared the square she began to tremble again, walking with her head up, her hands clenched at her sides, their voices about her murmurous, also with that feverish, glittering quality of their eyes.

They entered the square, she in the center of the group, fragile in her fresh dress. She was trembling worse. She walked slower and slower, as children eat ice-cream, her head up and her eyes bright in the haggard banner of her face, passing the hotel and the coatless drummers in chairs along the curb looking around at her: 'That's the one: see? The one in pink in the middle.' 'Is that her? What did they do with nigger? Did they—?' 'Sure. He's all right.' 'All right, is he?' 'Sure. He went on a little trip.' Then the drug store, where even the young men lounging in the doorway tipped their hats and followed with their eyes the motion of her hips and legs when she passed.

They went on, passing the lifted hats of the gentlemen, the suddenly ceased voices, deferent, protective. 'Do you see?' the friends said. Their voices sounded like long, hovering sighs of hissing exultation. 'There's not a Negro on the square. Not one.'

They reached the picture show. It was like a miniature fairyland with its lighted lobby and colored lithographs of life caught in its terrible and beautiful mutations. Her lips began to tingle. In the dark, when the picture began, it would be all right; she could hold back the laughing so it would not waste away so fast and so soon. So she hurried on before the turning faces, the undertones of low astonishment, and they took their accustomed places where she could see the aisle against the silver glare and the young men and girls coming in two and two against it.

The lights flickered away; the screen glowed silver, and soon life began to unfold, beautiful and passionate and sad, while still the young men and girls entered, scented and sibilant in the half dark, their paired backs in silhouette delicate and sleek, their slim, quick bodies awkward, divinely young, while beyond them the silver dream accumulated, inevitably on and on. She began to laugh. In trying to suppress it, it made more noise than ever; heads began to turn. Still laughing, her friends raised her and led her out, and she stood at the curb, laughing on a high, sustained note, until the taxi came up and they helped her in.

They removed the pink voile and the sheer underthings and the stockings, and put her to bed, and cracked ice for her temples, and sent for the doctor. He was hard to locate, so they ministered to her with hushed ejaculations, renewing the ice and fanning her. While the ice was fresh and cold she stopped laughing and lay still for a time, moaning only a little. But soon the laughing welled again and her voice rose screaming.

'Shhhhhhhhhhh! Shhhhhhhhhhh!' they said, freshening the icepack, smoothing her hair, examining it for gray; 'poor girl!' Then to one another: 'Do you suppose anything really happened?' their eyes darkly aglitter, secret and passionate. 'Shhhhhhhhhh! Poor girl! Poor Minnie!'

V

It was midnight when McLendon drove up to his neat new house. It was trim and fresh as a birdcage and almost as small, with its clean, green-and-white paint. He locked the car and mounted the porch and entered. His wife rose from a chair beside the reading lamp. McLendon stopped in the floor and stared at her until she looked down.

'Look at that clock,' he said, lifting his arm, pointing. She stood before him, her face lowered, a magazine in her hands. Her face was pale, strained, and weary-looking. 'Haven't I told you about sitting up like this, waiting to see when I come in?'

'John,' she said. She laid the magazine down. Poised on the balls of his feet, he glared at her with his hot eyes, his sweating face.

'Didn't I tell you?' He went toward her. She looked up then. He caught her shoulder. She stood passive looking at him.

'Don't, John. I couldn't sleep... The heat; something. Please, John. You're hurting me.'

'Didn't I tell you?' He released her and half struck, half flung her across the chair, and she lay there and watched him quietly as he left the room.

He went on through the house, ripping off his shirt, and on the dark, screened porch at the rear he stood and mopped his head and shoulders with the shirt and flung it away. He took the pistol from his hip and laid it on the table beside the bed, and sat on the bed and removed his shoes, and rose and slipped his trousers off. He was sweating again already, and he stooped and hunted furiously for the shirt. At last he found it and wiped his body again, and, with his body pressed against the dusty screen, he stood panting. There was no movement, no sound, not even an insect. The dark world seemed to lie stricken beneath the cold moon and the lidless stars.

Misty, Tiled Chambers

Valerie Miner

'Nine is old enough to learn to swim,' Mom said, letting me have the window seat on the bus.

'But *you* don't know how to swim,' I protested.

'Exactly!' she pronounced with the infallible logic she always used when refuting arguments with my own words.

Mom made me wear my heavy jacket and her own long, wool scarf. She wore the old red coat and her neck looked too long that morning. When I was mad at my mother I found fault with her appearance – especially with her skinny face and bow legs. I was furious with her today because it was 20 degrees outside and she was dragging me all the way to Hackensack for swimming lessons.

'But, Mom, it's too *cold* for a bathing suit. Why don't we wait for summer?'

'It's crowded in the summer. This way you'll be able to swim at the pond when the hot weather starts; won't that be nice?'

'I'd rather learn piano.'

She looked past me at snowmen guarding white lawns along Madison Avenue.

'Why can't I take piano? Jackie has lessons.'

'Music lessons are expensive, dear. Besides, you'd have to practise. We could hardly afford a *piano*.'

I stared at an icicle forming on a telephone wire. 'I could practise on Jackie's.' I looked back with expectation.

She was picking absentmindedly at a callus on her palm. It was about to bleed and I tapped her. 'No, don't do that; it's bad for you.'

She smiled, then peered out the window again. We were silent for the rest of the trip.

As we pulled into Hackensack, she took my hand, 'You'll like swimming. Give it a chance.'

The YMCA was an imposing building, but lacking the ornate drama of St Mary's Catholic School. Here I noticed one crucifix, no statues, a lot of plain windows and a big desk. A woman with kinky, blonde hair gave Mom a form and took some money. She nodded at me insincerely. Soon Mom was marching me down a dark corridor and I remembered a movie where ancient people sacrificed their children to the gods.

The locker-room had a green smell. It was hot and humid, like July. I caught a glimpse of a fat woman without any clothes, before Mom hauled me over to a stall and handed me the regulation suit. The dark blue knit material was scratchy and stank of disinfectant. I thought about Mom taking me to the doctor, telling me to get undressed and lie on the table while she stood by, tall and invulnerable in that horrid red coat. How could she wear a heavy coat in this muggy room? This wasn't the first time I had doubted her sanity. Maybe I could run away to Jackie's and sleep under the piano.

'Hurry along, dear we only have five minutes before we meet your teacher.'

Mitch was waiting for us outside the ladies' dressing-room. He was a tall man with red hairs on his chest and head. At first glance, he reminded me of Buster Crabbe. Shyly, I stared at the locker-room door. The italicized 'Ladies' was so much more adult than the block lettered 'Girls' marking the bathroom at school. 'Ladies.' I tilted my head at the same angle as the white letters. I would tell Jackie about this.

'How do you do?' Mitch had a broad smile, but I didn't register the rest of his face because he reached down to shake my hand. And I noticed that he had several fingers missing. I watched the goosebumps rise along my arm.

Mom nudged me. Maybe she saw, too, and we could go home now. Instead, she said, 'Say "How-do-you-do?", Gerry.'

I knew it was rude to stare at people's handicaps. I knew I should be too adult to mention it. And yet I imagined his hand sticking in my throat, right above the 'How-do-you-do?'

'Well, a lot of people are shy at first.'

I noticed he was talking to me rather than to my mother.

'You'll be fine once we get in the water. Shall we test the temperature?'

He took my hand and I tried not to *feel*, just as I would try not to smell when I went to the bathroom at the movies. Instead, I concentrated on the high, winding echoes of the Hackensack pool. For the first time I noticed that there was a whole class of swimmers in the far end – the deep end – of the water. Mitch nodded toward the wading section.

He turned gently to Mom. 'You'll want to sit up there,' he said, pointing to the bleachers. 'That way you won't get wet.'

Coward, I thought, as she found a seat and let the strange man lead me down the cold metal ladder. I soon forgot her when he showed me how to dunk my head in and out of the water. Then I experienced the miracle of floating. I hardly thought about his hand until he lead me back to my mother beneath the italicized 'Ladies' sign.

'A natural.' He patted my shoulder. 'Regular mermaid. See you next week, Gerry?'

'Oh, yes, next week,' I answered, surprised by my enthusiasm.

It was a very cold winter, but each week we took the bus to Hackensack. Once I had learned to dog-paddle, Mitch gradu ated me from the wading section. Every so often I would look up and see Mom watching closely and pretending to be brave. After the lesson she always took me to Woolworth's for an egg salad sandwich and a ginger ale. I had completely forgotten about the piano. I hardly saw Jackie any more because she spent so much time indoors, practising.

One night I dreamt I was sitting on the edge of the pool, dangling my feet. The water had turned black and I was singing, trying to entice the missing fingers to surface from the bottom of the water.

During the day, I tried not to think about Mitch's hand. I never mentioned it to Mom. At first I thought it would be impolite to talk about his handicap – for surely she must have noticed it too. Then I worried that she hadn't noticed and that if

I told her about the missing fingers, she would cancel the lessons. None of the reasons made sense, but it seemed important to remain silent. I succeeded in forgetting about Mitch's hand until the week we began diving lessons.

He took me to the deep end, dove in himself, cutting the water sharply, swimming underneath, graceful as a dolphin. He surfaced with a big smile. 'See how easy it is?'

'Sure.' I stood shivering, suddenly remembering this was late January and it was sleeting outside.

'Just try jumping first,' he called. 'I'll catch you.'

I stood there, bolstered by his smile. Then I glanced over at Mom's encouraging face. The air was an endless expanse; the water, I knew, would be worse, for it went down fourteen feet. Suddenly I jumped. Down. Down. I couldn't decide between terror and exhilaration, and then I was safe. Mitch was holding my hands; we were looking at each other, spluttering and laughing.

'Brave girl,' he said.

I laughed, pumped my feet up and down and held onto his hands. Suddenly I was conscious of the missing fingers and panicked about drowning.

'Don't worry.' He caught my frown. 'Just hold on and I'll swim us to shore.'

Those four feet were interminable as I struggled to keep afloat, to hide my revulsion, to keep from throwing up.

'There,' he said as we reached the safe metal ladder. 'It's a little early to knock off, but you've done a lot for one day.'

I nodded, not daring to meet his eyes, for he must have known the cause of my distress. 'Thank you, Mitch. See you... next Saturday.'

I couldn't eat the egg salad sandwich. When Mom asked what was wrong, I broke down and sobbed, finally managing to confess.

She regarded me carefully. She listened as all my fears spilled out. Did he have a kind of leprosy? Was it catching? Or polio? Sometimes the Salk vaccine didn't work and I knew kids got polio from swimming. Were the missing fingers dangerous?

Would he lose his grip and let me slip to the bottom of the pool? Mom patted my perfectly formed hand and reassured me that I was safe. She speculated on how he might have lost his fingers – in an industrial accident, in the war.

The war, I decided. That night, watching a World War II movie on TV, I imagined Mitch on the frontline, perhaps the scout who went ahead of other soldiers to clear the way for his buddies and in the process...

Sergeant Mitch taught me the crawl, the side-stroke, the breast-stroke, the elementary back-stroke. I still had trouble diving. But he was impressed with my progress and told Mom I was his best student.

I liked the side-stroke because I could see all around me. I would look up at the ceiling and consider the funny, yellow light pouring through the high windows. I liked to peer down the length of the pool and watch the fat lady doing her laps and the toddlers splashing each other. Searching the bleachers, I would wave to Mom, who smiled as I swam past her fears. When I looked up at her nowadays she seemed more relaxed. Some-times she even sat back in her seat with her feet out on the bench in front of her.

The side-stroke made me feel like a graceful machine or one of those scissor bugs at the pond. It always put me in a quiet mood. I found the back-stroke too slow just as I considered the crawl too fast. With the breast-stroke, I could fly, clearing a path through the cool water with my strong arms. Sometimes Mitch and I played tag and he would dare me to chase after his sleek shadow on the chlorine floor.

The locker-room felt more comfortable now. I watched steam weaving around the dented gray lockers and I imagined this mist as angelhair breathing from the naked female forms. Mom made me get dressed in the cubicle, but many swimmers, particularly the older women, weren't at all shy. The different shapes were fascinating: tall, lean women with tiny breasts; others with chubby legs and big tummies. Everyone with that triangle of fur above the legs. I had a big curiosity because my mother was always very modest about her own body. Despite Mom's efficient method of whisking me in and out of the dressing-room, I learned a lot. One woman always creamed her legs, slowly, as if she were putting on delicate silk stockings, her hands rising higher and higher until she almost touched the triangle. Everyone had a different system for attaching the bra – some would snap it in front and then ponderously turn the bra around before putting their arms through the straps. Others were astonishingly quick at hooking from behind. The bras came in all sorts – flimsy cheesecloth models like the one my friend Karen wore; lacy, black styles and large, white contraptions with metal supports which made me think of the hairshirts Sister Martin talked about. Maybe women saints wore metal under their breasts. I loved the mingling scents of talcum powder and deodorant and perfume. I eavesdropped on the ladies' quick conversations about gaining and losing weight, raising kids and shopping. By late February I was a regular; several women began to greet me by name.

Sister told us we could write about anything we liked, so I was surprised when she asked me to stay after school to discuss my essay on Mitch's swimming lessons.

'Sit here,' she said in that voice she reserved for serious talks. 'Is it true, what you've written in your paper?' she asked slowly.

I looked into her long face, relieved that I could reassure her it wasn't a lie, that I had, indeed, mastered four strokes although my diving was still giving me trouble.

'Very nice, dear. But is it true that you're taking lessons at the YMCA?'

'Yes, Sister,' I answered proudly. 'All the way in Hackensack. Every Saturday.'

She breathed deeply and looked at me with kindness. 'But what can your mother be thinking about? The YMCA is a *Protestant* organization.'

'Oh, I know that, Sister. There are no statues, anywhere. It's a very plain building. But the pool is pretty, with lots of blues and greens...' I stopped at her impassive face.

'Dear, remember what we learned in catechism class about the First Commandment. You shouldn't be participating in a Protestant organization.'

'Oh, I see,' I said, in that voice Mom used when she didn't want to make a decision right away and planned to talk with my father first.

She changed her tack. 'And swimming in the middle of winter? Hackensack is a long way to travel. Have you considered piano? Mrs Sullivan teaches piano in her home.'

'No.' I shrugged. 'Swimming is more useful.' The anger rose suddenly in my throat. 'Music requires too many fingers.'

Sister decided not to pursue this last point. She tapped my knee and said conclusively, 'Gerry, I'm afraid that you'll just have to stop going there.'

'I see.' I wasn't sure how convincing my neutrality was because I was concentrating on holding back the tears.

The next week Mom and I were back on the bus to Hackensack. Mom explained that Sister was mistaken. She couldn't have understood that I was just learning how to swim, that it involved no religious instruction.

I stared out at the gray slush and the lawns peeking through the snow. This was a moral crisis for me because I didn't want to displease God. I didn't want my attendance at the YMCA to damn me to hell – what good would swimming do me there? On the other hand, I loved that old building and my new friends in the locker-room. And Mitch.

'Don't worry,' Mom repeated. 'Trust me. Sister Martin means well, but sometimes the nuns are a little... innocent about the world. They could get lost in their rules and regulations.'

I shrugged, but I felt very grown up. Although Mom complained about the nuns to Dad, this was the first time she had ever said anything to me. I tried to conceal my satisfaction.

'Trust me. Wasn't I right about swimming being fun?'

That was the day I did it. I wasn't sure what had got into me. I walked out to the fourteen foot sign, put my head down and dove straight into the green water.

'Perfect,' Mitch called, treading gracefully, holding out his hands to congratulate me.

'Perfect,' Mom called from the bleachers.

'Perfect,' I surfaced, reaching eagerly for his hands.

All winter during my ninth year I took the long bus ride from Dumond to Hackensack. Through the snow I traveled to those misty, tiled chambers where I learned how not to drown.

The Catbird Seat

James Thurber

Mr Martin bought the pack of Camels on Monday night in the most crowded cigar store on Broadway. It was theatre time and seven or eight men were buying cigarettes. The clerk didn't even glance at Mr Martin, who put the pack in his overcoat pocket and went out. If any of the staff at F & S had seen him buy the cigarettes, they would have been astonished, for it was generally known that Mr Martin did not smoke, and never had. No one saw him.

It was just a week to the day since Mr Martin had decided to rub out Mrs Ulgine Barrows. The term 'rub out' pleased him because it suggested nothing more than the correction of an error – in this case an error of Mr Fitweiler. Mr Martin had spent each night of the past week working out his plan and examining it. As he walked home now he went over it again. For the hundredth time he resented the element of imprecision, the margin of guesswork that entered into the business. The project as he had worked it out was casual and bold, the risks were considerable. Something might go wrong anywhere along the line. And therein lay the cunning of his scheme. No one would ever see in it the cautious, painstaking hand of Erwin Martin, head of the filing department at F & S, of whom Mr Fitweiler had once said, 'Man is fallible but Martin isn't.' No one would see his hand, that is, unless it were caught in the act.

Sitting in his apartment drinking a glass of milk, Mr Martin reviewed his case against Mrs Ulgine Barrows, as he had every night for seven nights. He began at the beginning. Her quacking voice and braying laugh had first profaned the halls of F & S on March 7, 1941 (Mr Martin had a head for dates). Old Roberts, the personnel chief, had introduced her as the newly appointed special adviser to the president of the firm, Mr Fitweiler. The woman had appalled Mr Martin instantly, but he hadn't shown it. He had given her his dry hand, a look of studious concentration, and a faint smile. 'Well,' she had said, looking at the papers on his desk, 'Are you lifting the oxcart out of the ditch?' As Mr Martin recalled that moment, over his milk, he squirmed slightly. He must keep his mind on her crimes as a special adviser, not on her peccadillos as a personality. This he found difficult to do, in spite of entering an objection and sustaining it. The faults of the woman as a woman kept chattering on in his mind like an unruly witness. She had, for almost two years now, baited him. In the halls, in the elevator, even in his own office, into which she romped now and then like a circus horse, she was constantly shouting these silly questions at him. 'Are you lifting the oxcart out of the ditch? Are you tearing up the pea patch? Are you hollering down the rain barrel? Are you scraping around the bottom of the pickle barrel? Are you sitting in the catbird seat?'

It was Joey Hart, one of Mr Martin's two assistants, who had explained what the gibberish meant. 'She must be a Dodger fan,' he had said. 'Red Barber announces the Dodger games over the radio and he uses those expressions – picked 'em up down South.' Joey had gone on to explain one or two. 'Tearing up the pea patch' meant going on a rampage; 'sitting in the catbird seat' meant sitting pretty, like a batter with three balls and no strikes on him. Mr Martin dismissed all this with an effort. It had been annoying, it had driven him near to distraction, but he was too solid a man to be moved to murder by anything so childish. It was fortunate, he reflected as he passed on to the important charges against Mrs Barrows, that he had stood up under it so well. He had maintained always an outward appearance of polite tolerance. 'Why, I even believed you like the woman,' Miss Paird, his other assistant, had once said to him. He had simply smiled.

A gavel rapped in Mr Martin's mind and the case proper was resumed. Mrs Ulgine Barrows stood charged with willful, blatant, and persistent attempts to destroy the efficiency and system of F & S. It was competent, material, and relevant to review her advent and rise to power. Mr Martin had got the story from Miss Paird, who seemed always able to find things out. According to her, Mrs Barrows had met Mr Fitweiler at a party, where she had rescued him from the embraces of a powerfully built drunken man who had mistaken the president of F & S for a famous retired Middle Western football coach. She had led him to a sofa and somehow worked upon him a monstrous magic. The ageing gentleman had jumped to the conclusion there and then that this was a woman of singular attainments, equipped to bring out the best in him and in the firm. A week later he had introduced her into F & S as his special adviser. On that day confusion got its foot in the door. After Miss Tyson, Mr Brundage, and Mr Bartlett had been fired and Mr Munson had taken his hat and stalked out, mailing in his resignation later, old Roberts had been emboldened to speak to Mr Fitweiler. He mentioned that Mr Munson's department had been 'a little disrupted' and hadn't they perhaps better resume the old system there? Mr Fitweiler had said certainly not. He had the greatest faith in Mrs Barrows' ideas. 'They require a little seasoning, a little seasoning, is all,' he had added. Mr Roberts had given it up. Mr Martin reviewed in detail all the changes wrought by Mrs Barrows. She had begun chipping at the cornices of the firm's edifice and now she was swinging at the foundation stones with a pickaxe.

Mr Martin came now, in his summing up, to the afternoon of Monday, November 2, 1942 – just one week ago. On that day, at 3 p.m., Mrs Barrows had bounced into his office. 'Boo!' she had yelled. 'Are you scraping around the bottom of the pickle barrel?' Mr Martin had looked at her from under his green eyeshade, saying nothing. She had begun to wander about the office, taking it in with her great, popping eyes. 'Do you really need *all* these filing cabinets?' She had demanded suddenly. Mr Martin's heart had jumped. 'Each of these files,' he had said, keeping his voice even, 'plays an indispensable part in the system of F & S.' She had brayed at him, 'Well, don't tear up the pea patch!' and gone to the door. From there she had bawled, 'But you sure have got a lot of fine scrap in here!' Mr Martin could no longer doubt that the finger was on his beloved department. Her pickaxe was on the upswing, poised for the first blow. It had not come yet; he had received no blue memo from the enchanted Mr Fitweiler bearing nonsensical instructions deriving from the obscene woman. But there was no doubt in Mr Martin's mind that one would be forthcoming. He must act quickly. Already a precious week had gone by. Mr Martin stood up in his living room, still holding his milk glass. 'Gentlemen of the jury,' he said to himself, 'I demand the death penalty for this horrible person.'

The next day Mr Martin followed his routine, as usual. He polished his glasses more often and once sharpened an already sharp pencil, but not even Miss Paird noticed. Only once did he catch sight of his victim; she swept past him in the hall with a patronizing 'Hi!' At five-thirty he walked home, as usual, and had a glass of milk, as usual. He had never drunk anything stronger in his life – unless you could count ginger ale. The late Sam Schlosser, the S of F & S, had praised Mr Martin at a staff meeting several years before for his temperate habits. 'Our most efficient worker neither drinks nor smokes,' he had said. 'The results speak for themselves.' Mr Fitweiler had sat by, nodding approval.

Mr Martin was still thinking about that red-letter day as he walked over to the Schrafft's on Fifth Avenue near Forty-sixth Street. He got there, as he always did, at eight o'clock. He finished his dinner and the financial page of the *Sun* at a quarter to nine, as he always did. It was his custom after dinner to take a walk. This time he walked down Fifth Avenue at a casual pace. His gloved hands felt moist and warm, his forehead cold. He transferred the Camels from his overcoat to a jacket pocket. He wondered, as he did so, if they did not represent an unnecessary note of strain. Mrs Barrows smoked only Luckies. It was his idea to puff a few puffs on a Camel (after the rubbing-out), stub it out in the ashtray holding her lipstick-stained Luckies, and thus drag a small red herring across the trail. Perhaps it was not a good idea. It would take time. He might even choke, too loudly.

Mr Martin had never seen the house on West Twelfth Street where Mrs Barrows lived, but he had a clear enough picture of it. Fortunately, she had bragged to everybody about her ducky first-floor apartment in the perfectly darling three-story redbrick. There would be no doorman or other attendants, just the tenants of the second and third floors. As he walked along, Mr Martin realized that he would get there before nine-thirty. He had considered walking north on Fifth Avenue from Schrafft's to a point from which it would take him until ten o'clock to reach the house. At that hour people were less likely to be coming in or going out. But the procedure would have made an awkward loop in the straight threat of his casualness, and he had abandoned it. It was impossible to figure when people would be entering or leaving the house, anyway. There was a great risk at any hour. If he ran into anybody, he would simply have to place the rubbing-out of Ulgine Barrows in the inactive file forever. The same thing would hold true if there were someone in her apartment. In that case he would just say that he had been passing by, recognized her charming house, and thought to drop in.

It was eighteen minutes after nine when Mr Martin turned into Twelfth Street. A man passed him, and a man and a woman, talking. There was no one within fifty paces when he came to the house, halfway down the block. He was up the steps and in the small vestibule in no time, pressing the bell under the card that said 'Mrs Ulgine Barrows.' When the clicking in the lock started, he jumped forward against the door. He got inside fast, closing the door behind him. A bulb in a lantern hung from the hall ceiling on a chain seemed to give a monstrously bright light. There was nobody on the stair, which went up ahead of him along the left wall. A door opened down the hall in the wall on the right. He went toward it swiftly, on tiptoe.

'Well, for God's sake, look who's here!' bawled Mrs Barrows, and her braying laugh rang out like the report of a shotgun. He rushed past her like a football tackle, bumping her. 'Hey, quit shoving!' she said, closing the door behind them. They were in her living room, which seemed to Mr Martin to be lighted by a hundred lamps. 'What's after you?' she said. 'You're as jumpy as a goat.' He found he was unable to speak. His heart was wheezing in his throat. 'I – yes,' he finally brought out. She was jabbering and laughing as she started to help him off with his coat. 'No, no,' he said. 'I'll put it here.' He took it off and put in on a chair near the door. 'Your hat and gloves, too,' she said. 'You're in a lady's house.' He put his hat on top of the coat. Mrs Barrows seemed larger than he had thought. He kept his gloves on. 'I was passing by,' he said. 'I recognized – is there anyone here?' She laughed louder than ever. 'No,' she said, 'we're all alone. You're as white as a sheet, you funny man. Whatever *has* come over you? I'll mix you a toddy.' She started toward a door across the room. 'Scotch-and-soda be all right? But say, you don't drink, do you?' She turned and gave him her amused look. Mr Martin pulled himself together. 'Scotch-and-soda will be all right,' he heard himself say. He could hear her laughing in the kitchen.

Mr Martin looked quickly around the living room for the weapon. He had counted on finding one there. There were andirons and a poker and something in a corner that looked like an Indian club. None of them would do. It couldn't be that way. He began to pace around. He came to a desk. On it lay a metal paper knife with an ornate handle. Would it be sharp enough? He reached for it and knocked over a small brass jar. Stamps spilled out of it and it fell to the floor with a clatter. 'Hey,' Mrs Barrows yelled from the kitchen, 'are you tearing up the pea patch?' Mr Martin gave a strange laugh. Picking up the knife, he tried its point against his left wrist. It was blunt. It wouldn't do.

When Mrs Barrows reappeared, carrying two highballs, Mr Martin standing there with his gloves on, became acutely conscious of the fantasy he had wrought. Cigarettes in his pocket, a drink prepared for him – it was all too grossly improbable. It was more than that; it was impossible. Some-where in the back of his mind a vague idea stirred, sprouted. 'For heaven's sake, take off those gloves,' said Mrs Barrows. 'I always wear them in the house,' said Mr Martin. The idea began to bloom, strange and wonderful. She put the glasses on a coffee table in front of a sofa and sat on the sofa. 'Come over here, you odd little man,' she said. Mr Martin went over and sat beside her. It was difficult getting a cigarette out of the pack of Camels, but he managed it. She held a match for him, laughing. 'Well,' she said, handing him his drink, 'this is perfectly marvellous. You with a drink and a cigarette.'

Mr Martin puffed, not too awkwardly, and took a gulp of the highball. 'I drink and smoke all the time,' he said. He clinked his glass against hers. 'Here's nuts to that old windbag, Fitweiler,' he said, and gulped again. The stuff tasted awful, but he made no grimace. 'Really, Mr Martin,' she said, her voice and posture changing, 'you are insulting our employer.' Mrs Barrows was now all special adviser to the president. 'I am preparing a bomb,' said Mr Martin, 'which will blow the old goat higher than hell.' He had only had a little of the drink, which was not strong. It couldn't be that. 'Do you take dope or something?' Mrs Barrows asked coldly. 'Heroin,' said Mr Martin. 'I'll be coked to the gills when I bump that old buzzard off.' 'Mr Martin!' she shouted, getting to her feet. 'That will be all of that. You must go at once.' Mr Martin took another swallow of his drink. He tapped his cigarette out in the ashtray and put the pack of camels on the coffee table. Then he got up. She stood staring at him. He walked over and put on his hat and coat. 'Not a word about this,' he said, and laid an index finger against his lips. All Mrs Barrows could bring out was 'Really!' Mr Martin put his hand on the doorknob. 'I'm sitting in the catbird seat,' he said. He stuck his tongue out at her and left. Nobody saw him go.

Mr Martin got to his apartment, walking, well before eleven. No one saw him go in. He had two glasses of milk after brushing his teeth, and he felt elated. It wasn't tipsiness, because he hadn't been tipsy. Anyway, the walk had worn off all effects of the whiskey. He got in bed and read a magazine for a while. He was asleep before midnight.

Mr Martin got to the office at eight-thirty the next morning, as usual. At a quarter to nine, Ulgine Barrows, who had never before arrived at work before ten, swept into his office. 'I'm reporting to Mr Fitweiler now!' she shouted. 'If he turns you over to the police, it's no more than you deserve!' Mr Martin gave her a look of shocked surprise. 'I beg your pardon?' he said. Mrs Barrows snorted and bounced out of the room, leaving Miss Paird and Joey Hart staring after her. 'What's the matter with that old devil now?' asked Miss Paird. 'I have no idea,' said Mr Martin, resuming his work. The other two looked at him and then at each other. Miss Paird got up and went out. She walked slowly past the closed door of Mr Fitweiler's office. Mrs Barrows was yelling inside, but she was not braying. Miss Paird could not hear what the woman was saying. She went back to her desk.

Forty-five minutes later, Mrs Barrows left the president's office and went into her own, shutting the door. It wasn't until half an hour later that Mr Fitweiler sent for Mr Martin. The head of the filing department, neat, quiet, attentive, stood in front of the old man's desk. Mr Fitweiler was pale and nervous. He took his glasses off and twiddled them. He made a small, bruffing sound in his throat. 'Martin,' he said, 'you have been with us more than twenty years.' 'Twenty-two, sir,' said Mr Martin. 'In that time,' pursued the president, 'your work and your – uh – manner have been exemplary.' I trust so, sir,' said Mr Martin. 'I have understood, Martin,' said Mr Fitweiler, 'that you have never taken a drink or smoked.' 'That is correct, sir,' said Mr Martin. 'Ah, yes,' Mr Fitweiler polished his glasses. 'You may describe what you did after leaving the office yesterday, Martin,' he said. Mr Martin allowed less than a second for his bewildered pause. 'Certainly, sir,' he said. 'I walked home. Then I went to Schrafft's for dinner. Afterward I walked home again. I went to bed early, sir, and read a magazine for a while. I was asleep before eleven.' 'Ah, yes,' said Mr Fitweiler again. He was silent for a moment, searching for the proper words to say to the head of the filing department. 'Mrs Barrows,' he said finally, 'Mrs Barrows has worked hard, Martin, very hard. It grieves me to report that she has suffered a severe breakdown. It has taken the form of a persecution complex accompanied by distressing hallucinations.' 'I am very sorry, sir,' said Mr Martin. 'Mrs Barrows is under the delusion,' continued Mr Fitweiler, 'that you visited her last evening and behaved yourself in an – uh – unseemly manner.' He raised his hand to silence Mr Martin's little pained outcry. 'It is the nature of these psychological diseases,' Mr Fitweiler said, 'to fix upon the least likely and most innocent party as the – uh – source of persecution. These matters are not for the lay mind to grasp, Martin. I've just had my psychiatrist, Dr Fitch, on the phone. He would not, of course, commit himself, but he made enough generalizations to substantiate my suspicions. I suggested to Mrs Barrows, when she had completed her – uh – story to me this morning, that she visit Dr Fitch, for I suspected a condition at once. She flew, I regret to say, into a rage, and demanded – uh – requested that I call you on the carpet. You may not know, Martin, but Mrs Barrows had planned a reorganization of your department – subject to my approval, of course, subject to my approval. This brought you, rather than anyone else, to her mind – but again, this is a phenomenon for Dr Fitch and not for us. So, Martin, I am afraid Mrs Barrows' usefulness here is at an end. 'I am dreadfully sorry, sir,' said Mr Martin.

It was at this point that the door to the office blew open with the suddenness of a gas-main explosion and Mrs Barrows catapulted through it. 'Is the little rat denying it?' she screamed. 'He can't get away with that!' Mr Martin got up and moved discreetly to a point beside Mr Fitweiler's chair. 'You drank and smoked at my apartment,' she bawled at Mr Martin, 'and you know it! You called Mr Fitweiler an old windbag and said you were going to blow him up when you got coked to the gills on your heroin!' She stopped yelling to catch her breath and a new glint came into her popping eyes. 'If you weren't such a drab, ordinary little man,' she said, 'I'd think you'd planned it all. Sticking your tongue out, saying you were sitting in the catbird seat, because you thought no one would believe me when I told it! My God, it's really too perfect!' She brayed loudly and hysterically, and the fury was on her again. She glared at Mr Fitweiler. 'Can't you see how he has tricked us, you old fool? Can't you see his little game?' But Mr Fitweiler had been surreptitiously pressing all the buttons under the top of his desk and employees of F & S began pouring into the room. 'Stockton,' said Mr Fitweiler, 'you and Fishbein will take Mrs Barrows to her home. Mrs Powell, you will go with them.' Stockton, who had played a little football in high school, blocked

Mrs Barrows as she made for Mr Martin. It took him and Fishbein together to force her out of the door into the hall, crowded with stenographers and office boys. She was still screaming imprecations at Mr Martin, tangled and contradictory imprecations. The hubbub finally died out down the corridor.

'I regret that this has happened,' said Mr Fitweiler. 'I shall ask you to dismiss it from your mind, Martin.' 'Yes, sir,' said Mr Martin, anticipating his chief's 'That will be all' by moving to the door. 'I will dismiss it.' He went out and shut the door, and his step was light and quick in the hall. When he entered his department he had slowed down to his customary gait, and he walked quietly across the room to the W20 file, wearing a look of studious concentration.

A New England Nun

Mary E. Wilkins Freeman

It was late in the afternoon, and the light was waning. There was a difference in the look of the tree shadows out in the yard. Somewhere in the distance cows were lowing and a little bell was tinkling; now and then a farm-wagon tilted by, and the dust flew; some blue-shirted laborers with shovels over their shoulders plodded past; little swarms of flies were dancing up and down before the peoples' faces in the soft air. There seemed to be a gentle stir arising over everything for the mere sake of subsidence – a very premonition of rest and hush and night.

This soft diurnal commotion was over Louisa Ellis also. She had been peacefully sewing at her sitting-room window all the afternoon. Now she quilted her needle carefully into her work, which she folded precisely, and laid in a basket with her thimble and thread and scissors. Louisa Ellis could not remember that ever in her life she had mislaid one of these little feminine appurtenances, which had become, from long use and constant association, a very part of her personality.

Louisa tied a green apron round her waist, and got out a flat straw hat with a green ribbon. Then she went into the garden with a little blue crockery bowl, to pick some currants for her tea. After the currants were picked she sat on the back door-step and stemmed them, collecting the stems carefully in her apron, and afterwards throwing them into the hen-coop. She looked sharply at the grass beside the step to see if any had fallen there.

Louisa was slow and still in her movements; it took her a long time to prepare her tea; but when ready it was set forth with as much grace as if she had been a veritable guest to her own self. The little square table stood exactly in the center of the kitchen, and was covered with a starched linen cloth whose border pattern of flowers glistened. Louisa had a damask napkin on her tea-tray, where were arranged a cut-glass tumbler full of teaspoons, a silver cream-pitcher, a china sugar-bowl, and one pink china cup and saucer. Louisa used china every day – something which none of her neighbors did. They whispered about it among themselves. Their daily tables were laid with common crockery, their sets of best china stayed in the parlour closet, and Louisa Ellis was no richer nor better bred than they. Still she would use the china. She had for her supper a glass dish full of sugared currants, a plate of little cakes, and one of light white biscuits. Also a leaf of lettuce, which she cut up daintily. Louisa was very fond of lettuce, which she raised to perfection in her little garden. She ate quite heartily, though in a delicate, pecking way; it seemed almost surprising that any considerable bulk of the food should vanish.

After tea she filled a plate with nicely baked thin corn-cakes, and carried them out into the back-yard.

'Caesar!' she called, 'Caesar! Caesar!'

There was a little rush, and the clank of a chain, and a large yellow-and-white dog appeared at the door of his tiny hut, which was half hidden among the tall grasses and flowers. Louisa patted him and gave him the corn-cakes. Then she returned to the house and washed the tea-things, polishing the china carefully. The twilight had deepened; the chorus of the frogs floated in at the open window wonderfully loud and shrill, and once in a while a long sharp drone from a tree-toad pierced it. Louisa took off her green gingham apron, disclosing a shorter one of pink and white print. She lighted her lamp, and sat down again with her sewing.

In about half an hour Joe Dagget came. She heard his heavy step on the walk, and rose and took off her pink-and-white apron. Under that was still another – white linen with a little cambric edging on the bottom; that was Louisa's company apron. She never wore it without her calico sewing apron over it unless she had a guest. She had barely folded the pink and white one with methodical haste and laid it in a table-drawer when the door opened and Joe Dagget entered.

He seemed to fill up the whole room. A little yellow canary that had been asleep in his green cage at the south window woke up and fluttered wildly, beating his little yellow wings against the wires. He always did so when Joe Dagget came into the room.

'Good-evening,' said Louisa. She extended her hand with a kind of solemn cordiality.

'Good-evening, Louisa,' returned the man, in a loud voice.

She placed a chair for him, and they sat facing each other, with the table between them. He sat bolt-upright, toeing out his heavy feet squarely, glancing with a good-humored uneasiness around the room. She sat gently erect, folding her slender hands in her white-linen lap.

'Been a pleasant day,' remarked Dagget.

'Real pleasant,' Louisa assented, softly. 'Have you been haying?' she asked, after a little while.

'Yes, I've been haying all day, down in the ten-acre lot. Pretty hot work.'

'It must be.'

'Yes, it's pretty hot work in the sun.'

'Is your mother well today?'

'Yes, mother's pretty well.'

'I suppose Lily Dyer's with her now?'

Dagget colored. 'Yes, she's with her,' he answered, slowly.

He was not very young, but there was a boyish look about his large face. Louisa was not quite as old as he, her face was fairer and smoother, but she gave people the impression of being older.

'I suppose she's a good deal of help to your mother,' she said, further.

'I guess she is; I don't know how mother'd get along without her,' said Dagget, with a sort of embarrassed warmth.

'She looks like a real capable girl. She's pretty-looking too,' remarked Louisa.

'Yes, she is pretty fair looking.'

Presently Dagget began fingering the books on the table. There was a square red autograph album, and a Young Lady's Gift-Book which had belonged to Louisa's mother. He took them up one after the other and opened them; then laid them down again, the album on the Gift-Book.

Louisa kept eyeing them with mild uneasiness. Finally she rose and changed the position of the books, putting the album underneath. That was the way they had been arranged in the first place.

Dagget gave an awkward little laugh. 'Now what difference did it make which book was on top?' said he.

Louisa looked at him with a deprecating smile. 'I always keep them that way,' murmured she.

'You do beat everything,' said Dagget, trying to laugh again. His large face was flushed.

He remained about an hour longer, then rose to take leave. Going out, he stumbled over a rug, and trying to recover himself, hit Louisa's work-basket on the table, and knocked it on the floor.

He looked at Louisa, then at the rolling spools; he ducked himself awkwardly toward them, but she stopped him. 'Never mind,' said she; 'I'll pick them up after you're gone.'

She spoke with a mild stiffness. Either she was a little disturbed, or his nervousness affected her, and made her seem constrained in her effort to reassure him.

When Joe Dagget was outside he drew in the sweet evening air with a sigh, and felt much as an innocent and perfectly well-intentioned bear might after his exit from a china shop.

Louisa, on her part, felt much as the kind-hearted, long-suffering owner of the china shop might have done after the exit of the bear.

She tied on the pink, then the green apron, picked up all the scattered treasures and replaced them in her work-basket, and straightened the rug. Then she set the lamp on the floor, and began sharply examining the carpet. She even rubbed her fingers over it, and looked at them.

'He's tracked in a good deal of dust,' she murmured. 'I thought he must have.'

Louisa got a dust-pan and brush, and swept Joe Dagget's track carefully.

If he could have known it, it would have increased his perplexity and uneasiness, although it would not have disturbed his loyalty in the least. He came twice a week to see Louisa Ellis, and every time, sitting there in her delicately sweet room, he felt as if surrounded by a hedge of lace. He was afraid to stir lest he should put a clumsy foot or hand through the fairy web, and he had always the consciousness that Louisa was watching fearfully lest he should.

Still the lace and Louisa commanded perforce his perfect respect and patience and loyalty. They were to be married in a month, after a singular courtship which had lasted for a matter of fifteen years. For fourteen out of the fifteen years the two had not once seen each other, and they had seldom exchanged letters. Joe had been all those years in Australia, where he had gone to make his fortune, and where he had stayed until he made it. He would have stayed fifty years if it had taken so long, and come home feeble and tottering, or never come home at all, to marry Louisa.

But the fortune had been made in the fourteen years, and he had come home now to marry the woman who had been patiently and unquestioningly waiting for him all that time.

Shortly after they were engaged he had announced to Louisa his determination to strike out into new fields, and secure a competency before they should be married. She had listened and assented with the sweet serenity which never failed her, not even when her lover set forth on that long and uncertain journey. Joe, buoyed up as he was by his sturdy determination, broke down a little at the last, but Louisa kissed him with a mild blush, and said good-by.

'It won't be for long,' poor Joe had said, huskily; but it was for fourteen years.

In that length of time much had happened. Louisa's mother and brother had died, and she was all alone in the world. But greatest happening of all – a subtle happening which both were too simple to understand – Louisa's feet had turned into a path, smooth maybe under a calm, serene sky, but so straight and unswerving that it could only meet a check at her grave, and so narrow that there was no room for any one at her side.

Louisa's first emotion when Joe Dagget came home (he had not apprised her of his coming) was consternation, although she would not admit it to herself, and he never dreamed of it. Fifteen years ago she had been in love with him – at least she considered herself to be. Just at that time, gently acquiescing with and falling into the natural drift of girlhood, she had seen marriage ahead as a reasonable feature and a probable desirability of life. She had listened with calm docility to her mother's views upon the subject. Her mother was remarkable for her cool sense and sweet, even temperament. She talked wisely to her daughter when Joe Dagget presented himself, and Louisa accepted him with no hesitation. He was the first lover she had ever had.

She had been faithful to him all these years. She had never dreamed of the possibility of marrying any one else. Her life, especially for the last seven years, had been full of a pleasant peace, she had never felt discontented nor impatient over her lover's absence; still she had always looked forward to his return and their marriage as the inevitable conclusion of things. However, she had fallen into a way of placing it so far in the future that it was almost equal to placing it over the boundaries of another life.

When Joe came she had been expecting him, and expecting to be married for fourteen years, but she was as much surprised and taken aback as if she had never thought of it.

Joe's consternation came later. He eyed Louisa with an instant confirmation of his old admiration. She had changed but little. She still kept her pretty manner and soft grace, and was, he considered, every whit as attractive as ever. As for himself, his stent was done; he had turned his face away from fortune-seeking, and the old winds of romance whistled as loud and sweet as ever through his ears. All the song which he had been wont to hear in them was Louisa; he had for a long time a loyal belief that he heard it still, but finally it seemed to him that although the winds sang always that one song, it had another name. But for Louisa the wind had never more than murmured; now it had gone down, and everything was still. She listened for a little while with half-wistful attention; then she turned quietly away and went to work on her wedding clothes.

Joe had made some extensive and quite magnificent alterations in his house. It was the old homestead; the newly-married couple would live there, for Joe could not desert his mother, who refused to leave her old home. So Louisa must leave hers. Every morning, rising and going about among her neat maidenly possessions, she felt as one looking her last upon the faces of dear friends. It was true that in a measure she could take them with her, but, robbed of their old environments, they would appear in such new guises that they would almost cease to be themselves. Then there were some peculiar features of her happy solitary life which she would probably be obliged to relinquish altogether. Sterner tasks than these graceful but half-needless ones would probably devolve upon her. There would be a large house to care for; there would be company to entertain; there would be Joe's rigours and feeble old mother to wait upon; and it would be contrary to all thrifty village traditions for her to keep more than one servant. Louisa had a little still, and she used to occupy herself pleasantly in summer weather with distilling the sweet and aromatic essences from roses and peppermint and spearmint. By-and-by her still must be laid away. Her store of essences was already considerable, and there would be no time for her to distil for the mere pleasure of it. Then Joe's mother would think it foolishness, she had already hinted her opinion in the matter. Louisa dearly loved to sew a linen seam, not always for use, but for the simple, mild pleasure which she took in it. She would have been loath to confess how more than once she had ripped a seam for the mere delight of sewing it together again. Sitting at her window during long sweet afternoons, drawing her needle gently through the dainty fabric, she was peace itself. But there was small chance of such foolish comfort in the future. Joe's mother, domineering, shrewd old matron that she was even in her old age, and very likely even Joe himself, with his honest masculine rudeness, would laugh and frown down all these pretty but senseless old maiden ways.

Louisa had almost the enthusiasm of an artist over the mere order and cleanliness of her solitary home. She had throbs of genuine triumph at the sight of the window-panes which she had polished until they shone like jewels. She gloated gently over her orderly bureau-drawers, with their exquisitely folded contents redolent with lavender and sweet clover and very purity. Could she be sure of the endurance of even this? She had visions, so startling that she half repudiated them as indelicate, of coarse masculine belongings strewn about in endless litter; of dust and disorder arising necessarily from a coarse masculine presence in the midst of all this delicate harmony.

Among her forebodings of disturbance, not the least was with regard to Caesar. Caesar was a veritable hermit of a dog. For the greater part of his life he had dwelt in his secluded hut, shut out from the society of his kind and all innocent canine joys. Never had Caesar since his early youth watched at a woodchuck's hole; never had he known the delights of a stray bone at a neighbor's kitchen door. And it was all on account of a sin committed when hardly out of his puppyhood. No one knew the possible depth of remorse of which this mild-visaged, altogether innocent-looking old dog might be capable; but whether or not he had encountered remorse, he had encountered a full measure of righteous retribution. Old Caesar seldom lifted up his voice in a growl or a bark; he was fat and sleepy; there were yellow rings which looked like spectacles around his dim old eyes; but there was a neighbor who bore on his hand the imprint of several of Caesar's sharp white youthful teeth, and for that he had lived at the end of a chain, all alone in a little hut, for fourteen years. The neighbor, who was choleric and smarting with the pain of his wound, had demanded either Caesar's death or complete ostracism. So Louisa's brother, to whom the dog had belonged, had built him his kennel and tied him up. It was now fourteen years since, in a flood of youthful spirits, he had inflicted that memorable bite and with the exception of short excursions, always at the end of the chain, under the strict guardianship of his master or Louisa, the old dog had remained a close prisoner. It is doubtful if, with his limited ambition, he took much pride in the fact, but it is certain that he was possessed of considerable cheap fame. He was regarded by all the children in the village and by many adults as a very monster of ferocity. St George's dragon could hardly have surpassed in evil repute Louisa Ellis's old yellow dog. Mothers charged their children with solemn emphasis not to go too near him, and the children listened and believed greedily, with a fascinated appetite for terror, and ran by Louisa's house stealthily, with many sidelong and backward glances at the terrible dog. If perchance he sounded a hoarse bark, there was a panic. Wayfarers chancing into Louisa's yard eyed him with respect, and inquired if the chain were stout. Caesar at large might have seemed a very ordinary dog, and excited no comment whatever; chained, his reputation over-shadowed him, so that he lost his own proper outlines and looked darkly vague and enormous. Joe Dagget, however, with his good-humoured sense and shrewdness, saw him as he was. He strode valiantly up to him and patted him on the head, in spite of Louisa's soft clamor of warning, and even attempted to set him loose. Louisa grew so alarmed that he desisted, but kept announcing his opinion in the matter quite forcibly at intervals. 'There ain't a better-natured dog in town,' he would say, 'and it's downright cruel to keep him tied up there. Some day I'm going to take him out.'

Louisa had very little hope that he would not, one of these days, when their interests and possessions should be more completely fused in one. She pictured to herself Caesar on the rampage through the quiet and unguarded village. She saw innocent children bleeding in his path, she was herself very fond of the old dog, because he had belonged to her dead brother, and he was always very gentle with her; still she had great faith in his ferocity. She always warned people not to go too near him. She fed him on ascetic fare of corn-mush and cakes, and never fired his dangerous temper with heating and sanguinary diet of flesh and bones. Louisa looked at the old dog munching his simple fare, and thought of her approaching marriage and trembled. Still no anticipation of disorder and confusion in lieu of sweet peace and harmony, no forebodings of Caesar on the rampage, no wild fluttering of her little yellow canary, were sufficient to turn her a hair's breadth. Joe Dagget had been fond of her and working for her all these years. It was not for her, whatever came to pass, to prove untrue and break his heart. She put the exquisite little stitches into her wedding-garments, and the time went on until it was only a week before her wedding-day. It was a Tuesday evening, and the wedding was to be a week from Wednesday.

There was a full moon that night. About nine o'clock Louisa strolled down the road a litle way. There were harvest-fields on either hand, bordered by low stone walls. Luxuriant clumps of bushes grew beside the wall, and trees – wild cherry and old apple-trees – at intervals. Presently Louisa sat down on the wall and looked about her with mildly sorrowful reflectiveness. Tall shrubs of blueberry and meadow-sweet, all woven together and tangled with blackberry vines and horsebriers, shut her in on either side. She had a little clear space between. Opposite her, on the other side of the road, was a spreading tree; the moon shone between its boughs, and the leaves twinkled like silver. The road was bespread with a beautiful shifting dapple of silver and shadow; the air was full of a mysterious sweetness. 'I wonder if it's wild grapes?' murmured Louisa. She sat there some time. She was just thinking of rising, when she heard footsteps and low voices, and remained quiet. It was a lonely place, and she felt a little timid. She thought she would keep still in the shadow and let the persons, whoever they might be, pass her.

But just before they reached her the voices ceased, and the footsteps. She understood that their owners had also found seats under the stone wall. She was wondering if she could not steal away unobserved, when the voice broke the stillness. It was Joe Dagget's. She sat still and listened.

The voice was announced by a loud sigh, which was as familiar as itself. 'Well,' said Dagget, 'you've made up your mind, then, I suppose?'

'Yes,' returned another voice; 'I'm going day after tomorrow.'

'That's Lily Dyer,' thought Louisa to herself. The voice embodied itself in her mind. She saw a girl tall and full-figured, with a firm, fair face, looking fairer and firmer in the moonlight, her strong yellow hair braided in a close knot. A girl full of a calm rustic strength and bloom, with a masterful way which might have beseemed a princess. Lily Dyer was a favorite with the village folk; she had just the qualities to arouse the admiration. She was good and handsome and smart. Louisa had often heard her praises sounded.

'Well,' said Joe Dagget, 'I ain't got a word to say.'

'I don't know what you could say,' returned Lily Dyer.

'Not a word to say,' repeated Joe, drawing out the words heavily. Then there was silence. 'I ain't sorry,' he began at last, 'that that happened yesterday – that we kind of let on how we felt to each other. I guess it's just as well we knew. Of course I can't do anything any different. I'm going right on an' get married next week. I ain't going back on a woman that's waited for me fourteen years, an' break her heart.'

'If you should jilt her tomorrow, I wouldn't have you,' spoke up the girl, with sudden vehemence.

'Well, I ain't going to give you the chance,' said he; 'but I don't believe you would, either.'

'You'd see I wouldn't. Honor's honor, an' right's right. An' I'd never think anything of any man that went against 'em for me or any other girl; you'd find that out, Joe Dagget.'

'Well, you'll find out fast enough that I ain't going against 'em for you or any other girl,' returned he. Their voices sounded almost as if they were angry with each other. Louisa was listening eagerly.

'I'm sorry you feel as if you must go away,' said Joe, 'but I don't know but it's best.'

'Of course it's best. I hope you and I have got common-sense.'

'Well, I suppose you're right.' Suddenly Joe's voice got an undertone of tenderness. 'Say, Lily,' said he. 'I'll get along well enough myself, but I can't bear to think – You don't suppose you're going to fret much over it?'

'I guess you'll find out I sha'n't fret much over a married man.'

'Well, I hope you won't – I hope you won't, Lily. God knows I do. And – I hope – one of these days – you'll come across somebody else –'

'I don't see any reason why I shouldn't. Suddenly her tone changed. She spoke in a sweet, clear voice so loud that she could have been heard across the street. 'No, Joe Dagget,' said she. 'I'll never marry any other man as long as I live. I've got good sense, an' I ain't going to break my heart nor make a fool of myself; but I'm never going to be married, you can be sure of that. I ain't that sort of a girl to feel this way twice.'

Louisa heard an exclamation and a commotion behind the bushes; then Lily spoke again – the voice sounded as if she had risen. 'This must be put a stop to,' said she. 'We've stayed here long enough. I'm going home.'

Louisa sat there in a daze, listening to their retreating steps. After a while she got up and slunk softly home herself. The next day she did her housework methodically; that was as much a matter of course as breathing; but she did not sew on her wedding-clothes. She sat at her window and meditated. In the evening Joe came. Louisa Ellis had never known that she had any diplomacy in her, but when she came to look for it that night she found it, although meek of its kind, among her little feminine weapons. Even now she could hardly believe that she had heard aright, and that she would not do Joe a terrible injury should she break her troth-plight. She wanted to sound him without betraying too soon her own inclinations in the matter. She did it successfully, and they finally came to an understanding; but it was a difficult thing, for he was as afraid of betraying himself as she.

She never mentioned Lily Dyer. She simply said that while she had no cause of complaint against him, she had lived so long in one way that she shrank from making a change.

'Well, I never shrank, Louisa,' said Dagget. 'I'm going to be honest enough to say that I think maybe it's better this way; but if you'd wanted to keep on, I'd have stuck to you till my dying day. I hope you know that.'

'Yes, I do,' said she.

That night she and Joe parted more tenderly than they had done for a long time. Standing in the door, holding each other's hands, a last great wave of regretful memory swept over them.

'Well, this ain't the way we've thought it was all going to end, is it, Louisa?' said Joe.

She shook her head. There was a little quiver on her placid face.

'You let me know if there's ever anything I can do for you,' said he. 'I ain't ever going to forget you, Louisa.' Then he kissed her, and went down the path.

Louisa, all alone by herself that night, wept a little, she hardly knew why; but the next morning, on waking, she felt like a queen who, after fearing lest her domain be wrested away from her, sees it firmly insured in her possession.

Now the tall weeds and grasses might cluster around Caesar's little hermit hut, the snow might fall on its roof year in and year out, but he never would go on a rampage through the unguarded village. Now the little canary might turn itself into a peaceful yellow ball night after night, and have no need to wake and flutter with wild terror against its bars. Louisa could sew linen seams, and distil roses, and dust and polish and fold away in lavender, as long as she listed. That afternoon she sat with her needle-work at the window, and felt fairly steeped in peace. Lily Dyer, tall and erect and blooming, went past; but she felt no qualm. If Louisa Ellis had sold her birthright she did not know it, the taste of the pottage was so delicious, and had been her sole satisfaction for so long. Serenity and placid narrowness had become to her as the birthright itself. She gazed ahead through a long reach of future days strung together like pearls in a rosary, every one like the others, and all smooth and flawless and innocent, and her heart went up in thankfulness. Outside was the fervid summer afternoon; the air was filled with the sounds of the busy harvest of men and birds and bees; there were halloos, metallic clatterings, sweet calls, and long hummings. Louisa sat, prayerfully numbering her days, like an uncloistered nun.

The Ambitious Guest

Nathaniel Hawthorne

One September night a family had gathered round their hearth, and piled it high with the driftwood of mountain streams, the dry cones of the pine, and the splintered ruins of great trees that had come crashing down the precipice. Up the chimney roared the fire, and brightened the room with its broad blaze. The faces of the father and mother had a sober gladness; the children laughed, the eldest daughter was the image of Happiness at seventeen; and the aged grandmother, who sat knitting in the warmest place was the image of Happiness grown old. They had found the 'herb, heart's-ease,' in the bleakest spot of all New England. This family were situated in the Notch of the White Hills, where the wind was sharp throughout the year, and pitilessly cold in the winter; – giving their cottage all its fresh inclemency before it descended on the valley of the Saco. They dwelt in a cold spot and a dangerous one; for a mountain towered above their heads, so steep, that the stones would often rumble down its sides and startle them at midnight.

The daughter had just uttered some simple jest that filled them all with mirth, when the wind came through the Notch and seemed to pause before their cottage – rattling the door, with a sound of wailing and lamentation, before it passed into the valley. For a moment it saddened them, though there was nothing unusual in the tones. But the family were glad again when they perceived that the latch were lifted by some traveler, whose footsteps had been unheard amid the dreary blast which heralded his approach, and wailed as he was entering, and went moaning away from the door.

Though they dwelt in such a solitude, these people held daily converse with the world. The romantic pass of the Notch is a great artery, through which the life-blood of internal commerce is continually throbbing between Maine on one side, and the

Green Mountains and the shores of the St Lawrence, on the other. The stage-coach always drew up before the door of the cottage. The wayfarer, with no companion but his staff, paused here to exchange a word, that the sense of loneliness might not utterly overcome him ere he could pass through the cleft of the mountain, or reach the first house in the valley. And here the teamster, on his way to Portland market, would put up for the night; and, if a bachelor, might sit an hour beyond the usual bedtime, and steal a kiss from the mountain maid at parting. It was one of those primitive taverns where the traveler pays only for food and lodging, but meets with a homely kindness beyond all price. When the footsteps were heard, therefore, between the outer door and the inner one, the whole family rose up, grandmother, children, and all, as if about to welcome some one who belonged to them, and whose fate was linked with theirs.

The door was opened by a young man. His face at first wore the melancholy expression, almost despondency, of one who travels a wild and bleak road, at nightfall and alone, but soon brightened up when he saw the kindly warmth of his reception. He felt his fear spring forward to meet them all, from the old woman, who wiped a chair with her apron, to the little child that held out its arms to him. One glance and smile placed the stranger on a footing of innocent familiarity with the eldest daughter.

'Ah, this fire is the right thing!' cried he; 'especially when there is such a pleasant circle round it. I am quite benumbed; for the Notch is just like the pipe of a great pair of bellows; it has blown a terrible blast in my face all the way from Bartlett.'

'Then you are going towards Vermont?' said the master of the house, as he helped to take a light knapsack off the young man's shoulders.

'Yes; to Burlington, and far enough beyond,' replied he. 'I meant to have been at Ethan Crawford's to-night; but a pedestrian lingers along such a road as this. It is no matter for, when I saw the good fire, and all your cheerful faces, I felt as if you had kindled it on purpose for me, and were waiting my arrival. So I shall sit down among you, and make myself at home.'

The frank-hearted stranger had just drawn his chair to the fire when something like a heavy footstep was heard without, rushing down the steep side of the mountain, as with long and rapid strides, and taking such a leap in passing the cottage as to strike the opposite precipice. The family held their breath, because they knew the sound, and their guest held his by instinct.

'The old mountain has thrown a stone at us, for fear we should forget him,' said the landlord, recovering himself. He sometimes nods his head and threatens to come down; but we are old neighbors, and agreed together pretty well upon the whole. Besides we have a sure place of refuge hard by if he should be coming in good earnest.'

Let us now suppose the stranger to have finished his supper of bear's meat; and, by his natural felicity of manner to have placed himself on a footing of kindness with the whole family, so that they talked as freely together as if he belonged to their mountain brood. He was of a proud, yet gentle spirit – haughty and reserved among the rich and great; but ever ready to stoop his head to the lowly cottage door and be like a brother or a son at the poor man's fireside. In the household of the Notch he found warmth and simplicity of feeling, the pervading intelligence of New England, and a poetry of native growth, which they had gathered when they little thought of it from the mountain peaks and chasms, and at the very threshold of their romantic and dangerous abode. He had traveled far and alone; his whole life, indeed, had been a solitary path; for, with the lofty caution of his nature, he had kept himself apart from those who might otherwise have been his companions. The family, too, though so kind and hospitable, had that consciousness of unity among themselves, and separation from the world at large, which, in every domestic circle, should still keep a holy place where no stranger may intrude. But this evening a prophetic sympathy impelled the refined and educated youth to pour out his heart before the simple mountaineers, and constrained them to answer him with the same free confidence. And thus it should have been. Is not the kindred of a common fate a closer tie than that of birth?

The secret of the young man's character was a high and abstracted ambition. He could have borne to live an undistinguished life, but not to be forgotten in the grave. Yearning desire had been transformed to hope; and hope, long cherished, had become like certainty, that, obscurely as he journeyed now, a glory was to beam on all his pathway, – though not, perhaps, while he was treading it. But when posterity should gaze back into the gloom of what was now the present, they would trace the brightness of his footsteps, brightening as meaner glories faded, and confess that a gifted one had passed from his cradle to his tomb with none to recognize him.

'As yet,' cried the stranger – his cheek glowing and his eye flashing with enthusiasm – as yet, I have done nothing. Were I to vanish from the earth tomorrow, none would know so much of me as you: that a nameless youth came up at nightfall from the valley of the Saco, and opened his heart to you in the evening, and passed through the Notch by sunrise, and was seen no more. Not a soul would ask, 'Who was he? Whither did the wanderer go?' But I cannot die till I have achieved my destiny. Then, let Death come! I shall have built my monument!'

There was a continual flow of natural emotion, gushing forth amid abstracted reverie, which enabled the family to understand this young man's sentiments, though so foreign from their own. With quick sensibility of the ludicrous, he blushed at the ardor into which he had been betrayed.

'You laugh at me,' said he, taking the eldest daughter's hand, and laughing himself. 'You think my ambition as nonsensical as if I were to freeze myself to death on the top of Mount Washington, only that people might spy at me from the country round about. And, truly, that would be a noble pedestal for a man's statue!'

'It is better to sit here by this fire,' answered the girl, blushing, 'and be comfortable and contented, though nobody thinks about us.'

'I suppose,' said her father, after a fit of musing, 'there is something natural in what the young man says; and if my mind had been turned that way, I might have felt just the same. It is strange, wife, how his talk has set my head running on things that are pretty certain never to come to pass.'

'Perhaps they may,' observed the wife. 'Is the man thinking what he will do when he is a widower?'

'No, no!' cried he, repelling the idea with reproachful kindness. 'When I think of your death, Esther, I think of mine, too. But I was wishing we had a good farm in Bartlett, or Bethlehem, or Littleton, or some other township round the White Mountains; but not where they could tumble on our heads. I should want to stand well with my neighbors and be called Squire, and sent to General Court for a term or two; for a plain, honest man may do as much good there as a lawyer. And when I should be grown quite an old man, and you an old woman, so as not to be long apart, I might die happy enough in my bed, and leave you all crying around me. A slate gravestone would suit me as well as a marble one – with just my name and age, and a verse of a hymn, and something to let people know that I lived an honest man and died a Christian.'

'There now!' exclaimed the stranger; 'it is our nature to desire a monument, be it slate or marble, or a pillar of granite, or a glorious memory in the universal heart of man.'

'We're in a strange way, to-night,' said the wife, with tears in her eyes. 'They say it's a sign of something, when folks' minds go a wandering so. Hark to the children!'

They listened accordingly. The younger children had been put to bed in another room, but with an open door between, so that they could be heard talking busily among themselves. One and all seemed to have caught the infection from the fireside circle, and were outvying each other in wild wishes, and childish projects of what they would do when they came to be men and women. At length a little boy, instead of addressing his brothers and sisters, called out to his mother.

'I'll tell you what I wish, mother,' cried he. 'I want you and father and grandma'm, and all of us, and the stranger too, to start right away, and go and take a drink out of the basin of the Flume!'

Nobody could help laughing at the child's notion of leaving a warm bed, and dragging them from a cheerful fire, to visit the basin of the Flume, – a brook, which tumbles over the precipice, deep within the Notch. The boy had hardly spoken when a wagon rattled along the road, and stopped a moment before the door. It appeared to contain two or three men, who were cheering their hearts with the rough chorus of a song, which resounded, in broken notes, between the cliffs, while the singers hesitated whether to continue their journey or put up here for the night.'

'Father,' said the girl, 'they are calling you by name.'

But the good man doubted whether they had really called him, and was unwilling to show himself too solicitous of gain by inviting people to patronize his house. He therefore did not hurry to the door; and the lash being soon applied, the travelers plunged into the Notch, still singing and laughing, though their music and mirth came back drearily from the heart of the mountain.

'There, mother!' cried the boy, again. 'They'd have given us a ride to the Flume.'

Again they laughed at the child's pertinacious fancy for a night ramble. But it happened that a light cloud passed over the daughter's spirit; she looked gravely into the fire, and drew a breath that was almost a sigh. It forced its way, in spite of a little struggle to repress it. Then starting and blushing, she looked quickly round the circle as if they had caught a glimpse into her bosom. The stranger asked what she had been thinking of.

'Nothing,' answered she, with a downcast smile. Only I felt lonesome just then.'

'Oh, I have always had a gift of feeling what is in other people's hearts,' said he, half seriously. 'Shall I tell the secrets of yours? For I know what to think when a young girl shivers by a warm hearth, and complains of lonesomeness at her mother's side. Shall I put these feelings into words?'

'They would not be a girl's feelings any longer if they could be put into words,' replied the mountain nymph, laughing, but avoiding his eye.

All this was said apart. Perhaps a germ of love was springing in their hearts, so pure that it might blossom in Paradise, since it could not be matured on earth; for women worship such gentle dignity as his; and the proud, contemplative, yet kindly soul is oftenest captivated by simplicity like hers. But while they spoke softly, and he was watching the happy sadness, the lightsome shadows, the shy yearnings of a maiden's nature, the wind through the Notch took a deeper and drearier sound. It seemed, as the fanciful stranger said, like the choral strain of the spirits of the blast, who in old Indian times had their dwelling among these mountains, and made their heights and recesses a sacred region. There was a wail along the road, as if a funeral were passing. To chase away the gloom, the family threw pine branches on their fire, till the dry leaves crackled and the flame arose, discovering once again a scene of peace and humble happiness. The light hovered about them fondly, and caressed them all. There were the little faces of the children, peeping from their bed apart, and here the father's frame of strength, the mother's subdued and careful mien, the high-browed youth, the budding girl, and the good old grandam, still knitting in the warmest place. The aged woman looked up from her task, and, with fingers ever busy, was the next to speak.

'Old folks have their notions,' said she, 'as well as young ones. You've been wishing and planning; and letting your heads run on one thing and another, till you've set my mind a wandering too. Now what should an old woman wish for, when she can go but a step or two before she comes to her grave? Children, it will haunt me night and day till I tell you.'

'What is it, mother?' cried the husband and wife at once.

Then the old woman, with an air of mystery which drew the circle closer round the fire, informed them that she had provided her grave-clothes some years before – a nice linen shroud, a cap with a muslin ruff, and everything of a finer sort than she had worn since her wedding day. But this evening an old superstition had strangely recurred to her. It used to be said, in her younger days, that if anything were amiss with a corpse, if only the ruff were not smooth, or the cap did not set right, the corpse in the coffin and beneath the clods would strive to put up its cold hands and arrange it. The bare thought made her nervous.

'Don't talk so, grandmother!' said the girl, shuddering.

'Now,' – continued the old woman, with singular earnestness, yet smiling strangely at her own folly, – 'I want one of you, my children – when your mother is dressed and in the coffin – I want one of you to hold a looking-glass over my face. Who knows but I may take a glimpse at myself, and see whether all's right?'

'Old and young, we dream of graves and monuments,' murmured the stranger youth. 'I wonder how mariners feel when the ship is sinking, and they, unknown and undistinguished, are to be buried together in the ocean – that wide and nameless sepulchre?'

For a moment, the old woman's ghastly conception so engrossed the minds of her hearers that a sound abroad in the night, rising like the roar of a blast, had grown broad, deep, and terrible, before the fated group were conscious of it. The house and all within it trembled; the foundations of the earth seemed to be shaken, as if this awful sound were the peal of the last trump. Young and old exchanged one wild glance, and remained an instant, pale, affrighted, without utterance, or power to move. Then the same shriek burst simultaneously from all their lips.

'The Slide! The Slide!'

The simplest words must intimate, but not portray, the unutterable horror of the catastrophe. The victims rushed from their cottage, and sought refuge in what they deemed a safer spot – where, in contemplation of such an emergency, a sort of barrier had been reared. Alas! they had quitted their security, and fled right into the pathway of destruction. Down came the whole side of the mountain, in a cataract of ruin. Just before it reached the house, the stream broke into two branches – shivered not a window there, but overwhelmed the whole vicinity, blocked up the road, and annihilated everything in its dreadful course. Long ere the thunder of the great Slide had ceased to roar among the mountains, the mortal agony had been endured, and the victims were at peace. Their bodies were never found.

The next morning, the light smoke was seen stealing from the cottage chimney up the mountain side. Within the fire was yet smouldering on the hearth, and the hearth and the chairs in a circle round it, as if the inhabitants had but gone forth to view the devastations of the Slide, and would shortly return, to thank Heaven for their miraculous escape. All had left separate tokens, by which those who had known the family were made to shed a tear for each. Who has not heard their name? The story has been told far and wide, and will forever be a legend of these mountains. Poets have sung their fate.

There were circumstances which led some to suppose that a stranger had been received into the cottage on this awful night, and had shared the catastrophe of all its inmates. Others denied that there were sufficient grounds for such a conjecture. Woe for the high-souled youth, with his dream of Earthly Immortality! His name and person utterly unknown; his history, his way of life, his plans, a mystery never to be solved, his death and his existence equally a doubt! Whose was the agony of that death moment?

The Idea in the Back of My Brother's Head

William Saroyan

I could hear my brother every morning. Lying in bed half asleep, I knew he was working on the family Ford, because when I first heard the noise I got out of bed to see what it was. I saw old Henry at work on the motor of the Model-T Ford. I saw him remove a bolt from somewhere and look at it as if he'd expected to see something else. Then I saw him put the bolt on the patch of lawn between the sidewalk and the kerb where the car was parked. I saw him get out another bolt and look at this one as if it weren't exactly like the first one, and I said to myself: 'Old Henry, he's fixing that car up because he's got an idea in the back of his head.'

Henry was sixteen. I thought of him as old Henry not because I was thirteen but because he was a pal.

That first morning he worked so quietly I could barely hear him, and I almost didn't wake up. All day I wanted to know what it was old Henry had at the back of his head. When I got to the telegraph office that afternoon I said: 'What are you doing to the Ford, Henry?'

'Plugs.'

'What about 'em?'

'Car's a little slow getting away.'

Every morning the whole month I heard him working on the car, out in the street in front of our new house, on El Monte Way, across from the multimillionaire's square-block estate, with castle and gardens and a real peacock.

After he'd got going, three or four days after he'd started working at daybreak every morning, I began to hear the cry of the peacock, which up to that time I had heard only around sundown (if I happened to be home) or on Sundays.

One morning when I got up to have another look at old Henry and the work he was doing I saw the peacock at the edge of the multimillionaire's estate on the other side of the wire fence, an oleander tree on one side, a rose tree on the other, both trees loaded with flowers. Henry was standing in front of the car, looking at a piston as if it were one of the noblest achievements of contemporary art. He looked at it, and then he put it down beside a lot of other parts lying on the patch of lawn between the sidewalk and the kerb. The patch of lawn had become black from the oil on the parts, but most of the lawn was Bermuda grass anyway, and the roots of the sycamore tree ran all through the patch, so that it didn't matter if the grass was black. It wasn't ever real green, anyway, or real grass, either: it was a weed, working hard to make the lumpy surface into something like a carpet, the shoots mingling every which way and lying five or six inches deep all over one another.

Old Henry concentrated on everything he did. That morning he concentrated so hard he didn't notice that the multimillionaire's peacock had come over to the corner of the estate, right across the street. The peacock cried out again, but old Henry didn't turn to see what it was. The peacock cried out three times, and then it spread its tall feathers, strutting and showing off, and I was sure old Henry would turn and take a look, but he didn't. I thought I'd holler at him to look at the multimillionaire's peacock, but I decided not to, because it wasn't any of my business, and I wasn't sure old Henry wouldn't say: 'I already seen him.'

The red oldeander blossoms and the white roses on either side of the peacock with its tail fanned out was a sight to see, though, and I guess I just *had* to believe all that color and crying at a time of absolute silence in the world had something to do with me and my idea of getting out there in the world pretty soon and doing something. I went back to bed as glad as I could be, and that afternoon at the telegraph office I said to him: 'What are you doing to the Ford every morning, Henry?'

'Fixing it.'

Old Henry didn't say anything. I didn't want him to get the idea I was against whatever he was doing, so I said: 'I'd get up and help you, but I don't get to bed until after one, and I'm still sleepy at daybreak.'

'I don't need any help just now,' he said, 'but later on I'll let you help me lift the motor off the frame.'

'Don't forget.'

When Sunday came around somebody in the family brought up the matter of driving to Kings River for a picnic and somebody else asked why not, a perfect day for a picnic at the side of the river, but Henry and I, we just looked at each other. We didn't say anything. The rest of the family, three women, went to work on stuff for a picnic and I went out to the back yard with old Henry and I said: 'Can you drive them to Kings River?'

'No,' he said. 'I'm working on the car. Will you tell them?'

'Tell them it broke down and I'm fixing it to save the money it would cost to get a mechanic to fix it.'

I went back into the house, into the kitchen, and I told the rest of the family the news. Most of the picnic stuff was ready, so we had a picnic in the back yard instead of at the river.

The following Sunday the situation was the same, so the family had another picnic in the back yard. Old Henry asked me to give him a hand, and together we went to work trying to get the motor off the frame. The rest of the family gathered around to see what was going on. They offered to help, too, but old Henry said work like that wasn't for women. He and I tried some more, and then he saw that he hadn't removed one bolt. He wasn't willing to make this fact known to the women, so we both kept trying to lift the motor, anyway.

We worked very hard at the impossible job.

One of the women said: 'Henry, do you know how to repair a car?'

Henry said he did. He was asked if he had studied work like that, and he said he hadn't, but he was finding out all about it as he worked. I agreed with him that that was the way to find out, all right, because I believed that that was the way I was going to do it, too, when I got out there in the world. After a while my mother's Uncle Gotto and his two daughters came up to the house in a horse-drawn carriage, so the women went off to receive them and serve them refreshments. Old Henry went to work as fast as he could go on the last bolt, got it out, and then he and I tried to lift the motor out, just as Uncle Gotto came up.

'Let me see what you've got there,' he said.

We got the motor up, out, and on to the patch of lawn.

'That's the block,' old Henry said, 'and these are the parts that fit into it.' He waved a finger slowly at a very orderly display of everything that he'd been able to get out of the motor.

'What's that screaming?' Uncle Gotto said.

'Peacock.'

This time old Henry waved a finger in the direction of the multimillionaire's square-block estate across the street.

'Why is he screaming?'

'He's *got* to.'

The old man thought about this a moment, and then he said: 'Henry, do you know how to repair the motor of an automobile?'

I thought old Henry was going to say he did, but he said: 'I'm learning as I go along.'

'Good boy,' the old man said. He went back into the house, walking slowly and stopping when the peacock cried out again.

That whole month of August, one of the truly great months of the year, one of the wild and wonderful months of life, especially when you're thirteen or sixteen, I heard old Henry working every morning on the Ford. Early the next month he said he believed he was finished, and now all he had to do was get the block back where it belonged, and all the parts back into the block. The following Sunday we worked together and got the block back, and I thought the time had come to ask him straight out.

'Henry,' I said, 'what have you got in the back of your head?'

'San Francisco.'

'What about it?'

'I'm going to drive there.'

'What about me?'

'You're going with me.'

'When?'

'Beginning next Friday morning. I've already asked J.D. for Friday, Saturday, Sunday, Monday, and Tuesday for the both of us, and he said he'd see, but I know he'll give us both those five days.'

'Does the rest of the family know?'

'Not yet. I thought I'd tell them at the last minute. I've got about thirty dollars saved up, and I guess you've got something, too.'

'Six dollars, but I'll start saving some more right away.'

Out of his back pocket old Henry brought a grease-stained highway map of California, unfolded it, and traced our course with the finger he'd used to point at the dismantled motor and in the direction of the peacock.

'Here's Fresno,' he said. 'We get up here at three in the morning, have breakfast, get our stuff into the car, and drive north to Madera, and then Chowchilla, where we turn west and drive to Los Banos. We keep going west, but now we start to climb. We climb and keep climbing until we get to the top of Pacheco Pass. Then we keep going west, but downhill now straight to Gilroy. Then we turn north and head for San Jose, and from there we go to San Franciso.

'Keen,' I said. That was the word we said in those days.

Working steadily that Sunday afternoon old Henry got everything back in place, including the secret map and the hood. He went off about ten yards, turned, faced the car, and for about three minutes stood there looking at it. Then he got in and sat behind the wheel and pressed the starter. I heard the right kind of sound when he did that, but *after* he'd done it I didn't hear anything more. He pressed the starter again, the sound was right again, but again it was followed by no other sound. At that moment the multimillionaire's peacock cried out.

'They've got to do that,' Henry said. He got out of the car and went around to the back of it and got out the crank. He told me to sit behind the wheel and get ready to feed the motor gas just as soon as the plugs fired. I got in behind the wheel and got set and old Henry started spinning the crank, but the plugs didn't fire. When he was tired I went to work with the crank, but it didn't make any difference which of us was doing it, the motor wouldn't start.

'I've got that motor in perfect shape,' he said.

'All the wires and connections back in place?'

'Everything.'

'Why doesn't it start?'

'Stiff.'

He started cranking again, and then when it was my turn I cranked, and then he cranked, and then the women came out of the house, the three in our own family, and the two visiting, and the old man, Gotto, too, and everybody watched, and Henry sweated, and the peacock cried out some more. Henry lifted the hood and looked at the motor. It was real clean and handsome. The women all looked, too, and the old man as well, but old Henry didn't touch anything. He just put the hood back and started cranking again. At last the spectators went back into the house and Henry came over to where I was sitting, all set to feed the motor gas, and he said: 'Come on, let's go see Kluck.'

I knew what that meant. It meant Henry needed some help and was willing to own up to it, because Shag Kluckjian was the most famous mechanic in our whole word. We walked down El Monte as fast as we could go to Hazelwood. We cut across the Longfellow School grounds, where we had both done time, to the Santa Fé tracks, past E. Y. Foley's grape-packing house to San Benito Avenue, from there to L Street, and a block and a half up L to Kluck's house.

Kluck was sitting on the steps of the front porch, smoking a cigarette, because he was nineteen now and out of school and working for a living. His father was sitting beside him, smoking a cigarette, too, and it seemed as if they had been talking quietly when all of a sudden we'd showed up. Old Henry asked Kluck if he'd come over to our house and have a look at the family Ford, which wouldn't start. Kluck invited us to sit up front with him in his Ford, with his father in the back, for the ride, and we drove straight ahead to Ventura Avenue, and then on to our house.

Kluck took off the hood, tried the starter, tried cranking, listening, and then brought a whole boxful of tools out of his car and went to work. One of the women in our family came out and asked Kluck's father into the house for some refreshment, and pretty soon we heard the wooden sound of backgammon pieces being slapped on to a board as old Gotto and Kluck's father played the game. Kluck worked fast and you could see he knew what he was doing. Old Henry watched every move he made, but he didn't say anything, and neither did Kluck. About three hours later Kluck's father came out of the house, and with him was Uncle Gotto, who had lost to Kluck's father at backgammon and wanted the game to go on. Kluck told his father there was a good two or three hours' more work to do, so his father went back into the house, and we began to hear the noise of the game again. Around sundown the multimillionaire's peacock came over to the corner of the estate, right across the street from where we lived, and cried out three times and spread its tail and began strutting around. Kluck stopped work long enough to notice the proud bird, and he said: 'Take a look at her royal highness, will you?'

'*His*' old Henry said. 'They're male.'

'They *are*?' Kluck said. 'I always thought the ones that showed off were female. Goes to show you how mistaken a fellow can be about almost anything.'

Kluck didn't criticize anything old Henry had done to the motor of the car, but you could see he was a little amazed now and then at the mistakes that came to light as he took the whole motor to pieces again.

There must have been a lot of mistakes.

It was almost night and dark when Kluck finished, and the motor was working the way it was meant to work, and always had, in fact. We went inside where the dinner table was set, and we sat down and ate a big supper. After supper old Henry went out and got behind the wheel of the car that was working again, and I went out, too.

'Go get Kluck, will you?'

The three of us went for a drive in the family car, Kluck driving, and when we got out by the county fairgrounds old Henry stuck his hand in his back pocket and brought out a little wad of currency. He held it out to Kluck, who said: 'What's that, Henry?'

Kluck took the money without stopping the car, and I just couldn't help it, I got worried, because I knew that that was all the money old Henry had saved up for the idea he had in the back of his head. Kluck unfolded the currency and examined each piece, as he kept driving slowly. There were five fives and five ones, and Kluck said: 'Thirty dollars, Henry.'

I was about to put in my two cents' worth about all that money for about six hours of work in the shade, with something like a park across the street, and a peacock in the park showing its feathers and letting the world hear its voice, but I reminded myself that I was three years younger than my brother, and if he wanted to give Kluck thirty dollars for a job that couldn't be worth more than six, a dollar an hour, then of course that was his business, although he must be crazy, and would never get rich.

Kluck turned the car around slowly and drove back to the house on El Monte Way. I don't think anybody said more than three words all the way back. Everybody was standing on the front lawn, so we knew everybody was ready to go, and I said to myself: 'Good-bye, thirty bucks. Good-bye, San Francisco.' Old Henry was awful quiet. I knew he felt sad about the month of work he had done on the car that had cost him all the money he had in the world. Kluck thanked the women for their hospitality and he asked his father if he was ready to go.

His father said goodnight to the women and went to Kluck's car. Henry and I stood in front of our car, watching. Kluck got into his car and started the motor and I was about to tell old Henry I thought he was crazy when I saw Kluck get out of the car and walk over to Henry. He put the folded money back in Henry's hand and he said: 'You know, Henry, I been thinking so much about that crazy peacock I almost drove off with your money.'

'No,' old Henry said, 'that money's yours, Kluck.' But Kluck just smiled and went back to his car and drove away.

The following Friday morning we were up at three and ready to take off on the greatest adventure of our lives. The women of our family came out in the dark to see that we got the apple box full of food properly settled on the floor in the back of the Ford, and all the other things they believed we ought to have on the trip, and then at last old Henry put the car to moving. By the time we got to the Ventura corner of the multimillionaire's estate I heard the cry of the peacock three times, but when I mentioned it to old Henry he said he hadn't heard anything. I wondered if I had *imagined* I had heard it, because I was so excited about the great idea I had in the back of my head about getting out there in the great world and doing something unforgettable.

The Happiest I've Been

John Updike

Neil Hovey came for me wearing a good suit. He parked his father's blue Chrysler on the dirt ramp by our barn and got out and stood by the open car door in a double-breased tan gabardine suit, his hands in his pockets and his hair combed with water, squinting up at a lightning rod an old hurricane had knocked crooked.

We were driving to Chicago, so I had dressed in worn-out slacks and an outgrown corduroy shirt. But Neil was the friend I had always been most relaxed with, so I wasn't very disturbed. My parents and I walked out of the house, across the low stretch of lawn that was mostly mud after the thaw that had come on Christmas Day, and my grandmother, though I had kissed her goodbye inside the house, came out onto the porch, stooped and rather angry-looking, her head haloed by wild old woman's white hair and the hand more severely afflicted by arthritis waggling at her breast in a worried way. It was growing dark and my grandfather had gone to bed. 'Nev-er trust the man who wears the red necktie and parts his hair in the middle,' had been his final advice to me.

We had expected Neil since middle afternoon. Nineteen almost twenty, I was a college sophomore home on vacation; that fall I had met in a fine arts course a girl I had fallen in love with, and she had invited me to the New Year's party her parents always gave and to stay at her house a few nights. She lived in Chicago and so did Neil now, though he had gone to our high school. His father did something – sell steel was my impression, a huge man opening a briefcase and saying 'The I-beams are very good this year' – that required him to be always on the move, so that at about thirteen Neil had been boarded with Mrs Hovey's parents, the Lancasters. They had lived in Olinger since the town was incorporated. Indeed, old Jesse Lancaster, whose sick larynx whistled when he breathed to us boys his shocking and uproaring thoughts on the girls that walked past his porch all day long, had twice been burgess. Meanwhile Neil's father got a stationary job, but he let Neil stay to graduate; after the night he graduated, Neil drove throughout the next day to join his parents. From Chicago to this part of Pennsylvania was seventeen hours. In the twenty months he had been gone Neil had come east fairly often; he loved driving and Olinger was the one thing he had that was close to a childhood home. In Chicago he was working in a garage and getting his teeth straightened by the Army so they could draft him. Korea was on. He had to go back, and I wanted to go, so it was a happy arrangement. 'You're all dressed up,' I accused him immediately.

'I've been saying good-bye.' The knot of his necktie was loose and the corners of his mouth were rubbed with pink. Years later my mother recalled how that evening his breath to her stank so strongly of beer she was frightened to let me go with him. '*Your* grandfather always thought *his* grandfather was a very dubious character,' she said then.

My father and Neil put my suitcases into the trunk; they contained all the clothes I had brought, for the girl and I were going to go back to college on the train together, and I would not see my home again until spring.

'Well, good-bye, boys,' my mother said. 'I think you're both very brave.' In regard to me she meant the girl as much as the roads.

'Don't you worry, Mrs Nordholm,' Neil told her quicky. 'He'll be safer than in his bed. I bet he sleeps from here to Indiana.' He looked at me with an irritating imitation of her own fond gaze. When they shook hands goodbye it was with an equality established on the base of my helplessness. His being so slick startled me, but then you can have a friend for years and never see how he operates with adults.

I embraced my mother and over her shoulder with the camera of my head tried to take a snapshot I could keep of the house, the woods behind it and the sunset behind them, the bench beneath the walnut tree where my grandfather cut apples into skinless bits and fed them to himself, and the ruts in the soft lawn the bakery truck had made that morning.

We started down the half-mile of dirt road to the highway that, one way, went through Olinger to the city of Alton and, the other way, led through farmland to the Turnpike. It was luxurious, after the stress of farewell, to two-finger a cigarette out of the pack in my shirt pocket. My family knew I smoked but I didn't do it in front of them; we were all too sensitive to bear the awkwardness. I lit mine and held the match for Hovey. It was a relaxed friendship. We were about the same height and had the same degree of athletic incompetence and the same curious lack of whatever force it was that aroused loyalty and compliance in beautiful girls. There was his bad teeth and my skin allergy; these were being remedied now, when they mattered less. But it seemed to me the most important thing – about both our friendship and our failures to become, for all the love we felt for women, actual lovers – was that he and I lived with grand-parents. This improved both our backward and forward vistas; we knew about the bedside commodes and midnight coughing fits that awaited most men, and we had a sense of childhoods before 1900, when the farmer ruled the land and America faced west. We had gained a humane dimension that made us gentle and humorous among peers but diffident at dances and hesitant in cars. Girls hate boys' doubts; they amount to insults. Gentleness is for married women to appreciate. (This is my thinking then.) A girl who has received out of nowhere a gift worth all Africa's ivory and Asia's gold wants more than just humanity to bestow it on.

Coming onto the highway, Neil turned right toward Olinger instead of left toward the Turnpike. My reaction was to twist and assure myself through the rear window that, though a pink triangle of sandstone stared through the bare treetops, nobody at my house could possibly see.

When he was again in third gear, Neil asked, 'Are you in a hurry?'

'No. Not especially.'

'Schuman's having his New Year's party two days early so we can go. I thought we'd go for a couple hours and miss the Friday night stuff on the Pike.' His mouth moved and closed carefully over the dull, silver, painful braces.

'Sure,' I said. 'I don't care.' In everything that followed there was this sensation of my being picked up and carried.

It was four miles from the farm to Olinger, we entered by Buchanan Road, driving past the tall white brick house I had lived in until I was fifteen. My grandfather had bought it before I was born and his stocks became bad, which had happened in the same year. The new owners had strung colored bulbs all along the front door frame and the edges of the porch roof. Downtown the cardboard Santa Claus still nodded in the drug store window but the loudspeaker on the undertaker's lawn had stopped broadcasting carols. It was quite dark now, so the arches of red and green lights above Grand Avenue seemed miracles of lift; in daylight you saw the bulbs were just hung from a straight cable by cords of different lengths. Larry Schuman lived on the other side of town, the newer side. Lights ran all the way up the front edges of his house and across the rain gutter. The next-door neighbor had a plywood reindeer-and-sleigh floodlit on his front lawn and a snowman of papier-mâché leaning tipsily (his eyes were x's) against the corner of his house. No real snow had fallen yet that winter. The air this evening, though, hinted that harder weather was coming.

The Schumans' living room felt warm. In one corner a blue spruce drenched with tinsel reached to the ceiling; around its pot surged a drift of wrapping paper and ribbon and boxes, a few still containing presents, gloves and diaries and other small properties that hadn't yet been absorbed into the mainstream of affluence. The ornamental balls were big as baseballs and all either crimson or indigo; the tree was so well-dressed I felt self-conscious in the same room with it, without a coat or tie and wearing an old green shirt too short in the sleeves. Everyone else was dressed for a party. Then Mr Schuman stamped in comfortingly, crushing us all into one underneath his welcome, Neil and I and the three other boys who had showed up so far.

He was dressed to go out on the town, in a vanilla topcoat and silvery silk muffler, smoking a cigar with the band still on. You could see in Mr Schuman where Larry got the red hair and white eyelashes and the self-confidence, but what in the son was smirking and pushy was in the father shrewd and masterful. What the one used to make you nervous the other used to put you at ease. While Mr was jollying us, Zoe Loessner, Larry's probable fiancée and the only other girl at the party so far, was talking nicely to Mrs, nodding with her entire neck and fingering her Kresge pearls and blowing cigarette smoke through the corners of her mouth, to keep it away from the middle-aged woman's face. Each time Zoe spat out a plume, the shelf of honey hair overhanging her temple bobbed. Mrs Schuman beamed serenely above her mink coat and rhinestone pocketbook. It was odd to see her dressed in the trappings of the prosperity that usually supported her good nature invisibly, like a firm mattress under a bright homely quilt. Everbody loved her. She was a prime product of the county, a Pennsylvania Dutch woman with sons, who loved feeding her sons and who imagined that the entire world, like her life, was going well. I never saw her not smile, except at her husband. At last she moved him into the outdoors. He turned at the threshold and did a trick with his knees and called in to us, 'Be good and if you can't be good, be careful.'

With them out of the way, the next item was getting liquor. It was a familiar business. Did anybody have a forged driver's license? If not, who would dare to forge theirs? Larry could provide India ink. Then again, Larry's older brother Dale might be home and would go straight from work to his fiancées apartment and stayed until Sunday. If worse came to worse, Larry knew an illegal place in Alton, but they really soaked you. The problem was solved strangely. More people were arriving all the time and one of them, Cookie Behn, who had been held back one year and hence was deposited in our grade, announced that last November he had become in honest fact twenty-one. I at least gave Cookie my share of the money feeling a little queasy, vice had become so handy.

The party was the party I had been going to all my life, beginning with Ann Mahlon's first Hallowe'en party, that I attended as hot, lumbering, breathless, and blind Donald Duck. My mother had made the costume, and the eyes kept slipping, and were further apart than my eyes, so that even when the clouds of gauze parted, it was to reveal the frustrating depthless world seen with one eye. Ann, who because her mother loved her so much as a child had remained somewhat childish, and I and another boy and girl who were not involved in any romantic crisis went down into Schuman's basement to play circular pingpong. Armed with paddles, we stood each at a side of the table and when the ball was stroked ran around it counter-clockwise, slapping the ball and screaming. To run better the girls took off their heels and ruined their stockings on the cement floor. Their faces and arms and shoulder sections became flushed, and when a girl lunged forward toward the net the stiff neckline of her semi-formal dress dropped away and the white arcs of her brassiere could be glimpsed cupping fat, and when she reached high her shaved armpit gleamed like a bit of chicken skin. An earring of Ann's flew off and the two connected rhinestones skidded to lie near the wall, among the Schumans' power mower and badminton poles and empty bronze motor-oil cans twice punctured by triangles. All these images were immediately lost in the whirl of our running; we were dizzy before we stopped. Ann leaned on me getting back into her shoes.

When we pushed it open the door leading down into the cellar banged against the newel post of the carpeted stairs going to the second floor; a third of the way up these, a couple sat discussing. The girl, Jacky Iselin, cried without emotion – the tears and nothing else, like water flowing over wood. Some people were in the kitchen mixing drinks and making noise. In the living room others danced to records: 78s then, stiff discs stacked in a ponderous leaning cylinder on the spindle of the Schumans' console. Every three minutes with a lick and a crash another dropped and the mood abruptly changed. One moment it would be 'Stay As Sweet As You Are'; Clarence Lang with the absolute expression of an idiot standing and rocking monotonously with June Kaufmann's boneless sad brown hand trapped in his and their faces, staring in the same direction, pasted together like the facets of an idol. The music stopped; when they parted, a big squarish dark patch stained the cheek of each. Then the next moment it would be Goodman's 'Loch Lomond' or 'Cherokee' and nobody but Margaret Lento wanted to jitterbug. Mad, she danced by herself, swinging her head recklessly and snapping her backside; a corner of her skirt flipped a Christmas ball onto the rug, where it collapsed into a hundred convex reflectors. Female shoes were scattered in innocent pairs about the room. Some were flat, resting under the sofa shyly toed in; others were high heels lying cockeyed, the spike of one thrust into its mate. Sitting alone and ignored in a great armchair, I experienced within a warm keen dishevelment, as if there were real tears in my eyes. Had things been less unchanged they would have seemed less tragic. But the girls who had stepped out of these shoes were with few exceptions the ones who had attended my life's party. The alterations were so small: a haircut, an engagement ring, a franker plumpness. While they wheeled above me I sometimes caught from their faces an unfamiliar glint, off of a hardness I did not remember, as if beneath their skins these girls were growing more dense. The brutality added to the features of the boys I knew seemed a more willed efect, more desired and so less grievous. Considering that there was a war, surprisingly many were present, 4-F or at college or simply waiting to be called. Shortly before midnight the door rattled and there, under the porchlight, looking forlorn and chilled in their brief athletic jackets, stood three members of the class ahead of ours who in the old days always tried to crash Schuman's parties. At Olinger High they had been sports stars, and they still stood with that well-coordinated looseness, a look of dangling from strings. The three of them had enrolled together at Melanchthon, a small Lutheran college on the edge of Alton, and in this season played on the Melanchthon basketball team. That is, two did; the third hadn't been good enough. Schuman, out of cowardice more than mercy, let them in, and they hid without hesitation in the basement, and didn't bother us, having brought their own bottle.

There was one novel awkwardness. Darryl Bechtel had married Emmy Johnson and the couple came. Darryl had worked in his father's greenhouse and was considered dull; it was Emmy that we knew. At first no one danced with her, and Darryl didn't know how, but then Schuman, perhaps as host, dared. Others followed, but Schuman had her in his arms most often, and at midnight, when we were pretending the new year began, he kissed her; a wave of kissing swept the room now, and everyone struggled to kiss Emmy. Even I did. There was something about her being married that made it extraordinary. Her cheeks in flame, she kept glancing for rescue, but Darryl, embarrassed to see his wife dance, had gone into old man Schuman's den, where Neil sat brooding, sunk in mysterious sorrow.

When the kissing subsided and Darryl emerged, I went in to see Neil. He was holding his face in his hands and tapping his foot to a record playing on Mr Schuman's private phonograph: Krupa's 'Dark Eyes.' The arrangement was droning and circular and Neil had kept the record going for hours. He loved saxophones; I guess all of us children of that Depression vintage did. I asked him, 'Do you think the traffic on the Turnpike has died down by now?'

He took down the tall glass from the cabinet beside him and took a convincing swallow. His face from the side seemed lean and somewhat blue. 'Maybe,' he said, staring at the ice cubes submerged in the ochre liquid. 'The girl in Chicago's expecting you?'

'Well, yeah, but we can call and let her know, once *we* know.'

'You think she'll spoil?'

'How do you mean?'

'I mean, won't you be seeing her all the time after we get there? Aren't you going to marry her?'

'I have no idea. I might.'

'Well then: you'll have the rest of Kingdom Come to see her.' He looked directly at me, and it was plain in the blur of his eyes

125

that he was sick-drunk. 'The trouble with you guys that have all the luck,' he said slowly, 'is that you don't give a f... about us that don't have any.' Such melodramatic rudeness coming from Neil surprised me, as had his blarney with my mother hours before. In trying to evade his wounded stare, I discovered there was another person in the room: a girl sitting with her shoes on, reading *Holiday*. Though she held the magazine in front of her face I knew from her clothes and her unfamiliar legs that she was the girl-friend Margaret Lento had brought. Margaret didn't come from Olinger but from Riverside, a section of Alton, not a suburb. She had met Larry Schuman at a summer job in a restaurant and for the rest of high school they had more or less gone together. Since then, though, it had dawned on Mr and Mrs Schuman that even in a democracy distinctions exist, probably welcome news to Larry. In the cruellest and most stetched-out way he could manage he had been breaking off with her throughout the year now nearly ended. I had been surprised to find her at this party. Obviously she had felt shaky about attending and had brought the friend as the only kind of protection she could afford. The other girl was acting just like a hired guard.

There being no answers to Neil, I went into the living room, where Margaret, insanely drunk, was throwing herself as if wanting to break a bone. Somewhat in time to the music she would run a few steps, then snap her body like a whip, her chin striking her chest and her hands flying backward, fingers fanned, as her shoulders pitched forward. In her state her body was childishly plastic; unharmed, she would bounce back from this jolt and begin to clap and kick and hum. Schuman stayed away from her. Margaret was small, not more than 5'3", with the smallness ripeness comes to early. She had bleached a section of her black hair platinum, cropped her head all over, and trained the stubble into short hyacinthine curls like those on antique statues of boys. Her face seemed quite coarse from the front, so her profile was classical unexpectedly. She might have been Portia. When she was not putting on her savage pointless dance she was in the bathroom being sick. The pity and the vulgarity of her exhibition made everyone who was sober uncomfortable; our common guilt in witnessing this girl's rites brought us so close together in that room that it seemed never, not in all time, could we be parted. I myself was perfectly sober. I had the impression then that people only drank to stop being unhappy and I nearly always felt at least fairly happy.

Luckily, Margaret was in a sick phase around one o'clock, when the elder Schumans came home. They looked in at us briefly. It was a pleasant joke to see in their smiles that, however corrupt and unwinking we felt, to them we looked young and sleepy: Larry's friends. Things quieted after they went up the stairs. In half an hour people began coming out of the kitchen balancing cups of coffee. By two o'clock four girls stood in aprons at Mrs Schuman's sink, and others were padding back and forth carrying glasses and ashtrays. Another blameless racket pierced the clatter in the kitchen. Out on the cold grass the three Melanchthon athletes had set up the badminton net and in the faint glow given off by the house were playing. The bird, ascending and descending through uneven bars of light, glimmered like a firefly. Now that the party was dying Neil's apathy seemed deliberately exasperating, even vindictive. For at least another hour he persisted in hearing 'Dark Eyes' over and over again, holding his head and tapping his foot. The entire scene in the den had developed a fixity that was uncanny; the girl remained in the chair and read magazines, *Holiday* and *Esquire*, one after another. In the meantime, cars came and went and raced their motors out front; Schuman took Ann Mahlon off and didn't come back; and the athletes carried the neighbor's artificial snowman into the center of the street and disappeared. Somehow in the arrangments shuffled together at the end, Neil had contracted to drive Margaret and the other girl home. Margaret convalesced in the downstairs bathroom for most of that hour. I unlocked a little glass bookcase ornamenting a desk in the dark dining room and removed a volume of Thackeray's Works. It turned out to be Volume II of *Henry Esmond*. I began it, rather than break another book out of the set, which had been squeezed in there so long the bindings had sort of inter-penetrated.

Henry was going off to war again when Neil appeared in the archway and said, 'O.K., Norseman. Let's go to Chicago.' 'Norseman' was a variant of my name he used only when feeling special affection.

We turned off all the lamps and left the hall bulb burning against Larry's return. Margaret Lento seemed chastened. Neil gave her his arm and led her back seat of his father's car; I stood aside to let the other girl get in with her, but Neil indicated that I should. I suppose he realized this left only the mute den-girl to go up front with him. She sat well over on her side, was all I noticed. Neil backed into the street and with unusual care steered past the snowman. Our headlights made vivid the fact that the snowman's back was a hollow right-angled gash; he had been built up against the corner of a house.

From Olinger, Riverside was diagonally across Alton. The city was sleeping as we drove through it. Most of the stoplights were blinking green. Among cities Alton had a bad reputation; its graft and gambling and easy juries and bawdy houses were supposedly notorious throughout the Middle Atlantic states. But to me it always presented an innocent face; row after row of houses built of a local dusty-red brick the shade of flowerpots, each house fortified with a tiny, intimate, balustraded porch, and nothing but the wealth of movie houses and beer signs along its main street to suggest that its citizens loved pleasure more than the run of mankind. Indeed, as we moved at moderate speed down these hushed streets bordered with parked cars, a limestone church bulking at every corner and the hooded street lamps keeping watch from above, Alton seemed less the ultimate center of an urban region than itself a suburb of some vast mythical metropolis, like Pandemonium or Paradise. I was conscious of evergreen wreaths on door after door and of fanlights of stained glass in which the house number was embedded. I was also conscious that every block was one block further from the Turnpike.

Riverside, fitted into the bends of the Schuylkill, was not so regularly laid out. Margaret's house was one of a short row, composition-shingled, which we approached from the rear, down a tiny cement alley speckled with drains. The porches were a few inches higher than the alley. Margaret asked us if we wanted to come in for a cup of coffee, since we were going to Chicago; Neil accepted by getting out of the car and slamming his door. The noise filled the alley, alarming me. I wondered at the easy social life that evidently existed among my friends at three-thirty in the morning. Margaret did, however, lead us in stealthily, and she turned on only the kitchen switch. The kitchen was divided from the living room by a large sofa, which faced into littered gloom where distant light from beyond the alley spilled over the window sill and across the spines of a radiator. In one corner the glass of a television set showed; the screen would seem absurdly small now, but then it seemed disproportionately elegant. The shabbiness everywhere would not have struck me so definitely if I hadn't just come from Schuman's place. Neil and the other girl sat on the sofa; Margaret held a match to a gas burner and, as the blue flame licked an old kettle, doled instant coffee into four flowered cups.

Some man who had once lived in this house had built by the kitchen's one window a breakfast nook, nothing more than a booth, a table between two high-backed benches. I sat in it and read all the words I could see: 'Salt,' 'Pepper,' 'Have some Lumps,' 'December,' 'Mohn's Milk, Inc. – A Very Merry Christmas and Joyous New Year – Mohn's Milk is *Safe* Milk – Mommy, Make it Mohn's!' 'Matches,' 'Hotpoint,' 'PRESS,' 'Magee Stove FEDERAL & Furnace Corp.,' 'God Is In This House,' 'Ave Maria Gratia Plena,' 'SHREDDED WHEAT Benefits Exciting New Pattern KUNGSHOLM'. After serving the two on the sofa, Margaret came to me with coffee and sat down opposite me in the booth. Fatigue had raised two blue welts beneath her eyes.

'Well,' I asked her, 'did you have a good time?'

She smiled and glanced down and made the small sound 'Ch,' vistigal of 'Jesus.' With absent-minded delicacy she stirred her coffee, lifting and replacing the spoon without a ripple.

'Rather odd at the end,' I said, 'not even the host there.'

'He took Ann Mahlon home.'

'I know.' I was surprised that she knew, having been sick in the bathroom for that hour.

'You sound jealous,' she added.

'Who does? I do? I don't.

'You like her, John, don't you?' Her using my first name and the quality of the question did not, although discounting parties we had just met, seem forward, considering the hour and that she had brought me coffee. There is very little further to go with a girl who has brought you coffee.

'Oh, I like everybody,' I told her, 'and the longer I've known them the more I like them, because the more they're me. The only people I like better are ones I've just met. Now Ann Mahlon I've known since kindergarten. Every day her mother used to bring her to the edge of the schoolyard for months after all the other mothers had stopped.' I wanted to cut a figure in Margaret's eyes, but they were too dark. Stoically she had gotten on top of her weariness, but it was growing bigger under her.

'Did you like her then?'

'I felt sorry for her being embarrased by her mother.'

She asked me, 'What was Larry like when he was little?'

'Oh, bright. Kind of mean.'

'Was he mean?'

'I'd say so. Yes. In some grade or other he and I began to play chess together. I always won until secretly he took lessons from a man his parents knew and read strategy books.'

Margaret laughed, genuinely pleased. 'Then did he win?'

'Once. After that I really tried, and after *that* he decided chess was kid stuff. Besides, I was used up. He'd have these runs on people where you'd be down at his house every afternoon, then in a couple months he'd get a new pet and that'd be that.'

'He's funny,' she said. 'He has a kind of cold mind. He decides on what he wants, then he does what he has to do, you know, and nothing anybody says can change him.'

'He does tend to get what he wants,' I admitted guardedly, realizing that to her this meant her. Poor bruised little girl, in her mind he was all the time cleaving with rare cunning through his parents' objections straight to her.

My coffee was nearly gone, so I glanced towards the sofa in the other room. Neil and the girl had sunk out of sight behind its back. Before this it had honestly not occurred to me that they had a relationship, but now that I saw, it seemed plausible and, at this time of night, good news, though it meant we would not be going to Chicago yet.

So I talked to Margaret about Larry, and she responded, showing really quite an accute sense of him. To me, considering so seriously the personality of a childhood friend, as if overnight he had become a factor in the world, seemed disproportionate; I couldn't deeply believe that even in her world he mattered much. Larry Schuman, in little more than a year, had become nothing to me. The important thing, rather than the subject, was the conversation itself, the quick agreements, the slow nods, the weave of different memories; it was like one of those Panama baskets shaped underwater around a worthless stone.

She offered me more coffee. When she returned with it, she sat down, not opposite, but beside me, lifting me to such a pitch of gratitude and affection the only way I could think to express it was by *not* kissing her, as if a kiss were another piece of abuse women suffered. She said, 'Cold. Cheap bastard turns the thermostat down to sixty,' meaning her father. She drew my arm around her shoulders and folded my hand around her bare forearm to warm it. The back of my thumb fitted against the curve of one breast. Her head went into the hollow where my arm and chest joined; she was terribly small, measured against your own body. Perhaps she weighed a hundred pounds. Her lids lowered and I kissed her two beautiful eyebrows and then the spaces of skin between the rough curls, some black and some bleached, that fringed her forehead. Other than this I tried to keep as still as a bed would be. It *had* grown cold. A shiver starting on the side away from her would twitch my shoulders when I tried to repress it; she would frown and unconsciously draw my arm tighter. No one had switched the kitchen light off. On Margaret's foreshortened upper lip there seemed to be two pencil marks; the length of wrist my badly fitting sleeve exposed looked pale and naked against the spiraling down of the smaller arm held beneath it.

Outside on the street the house faced there was no motion. Only once did a car go by: around five o'clock, with twin mufflers, the radio on and a boy yelling. Neil and the girl murmured together incessantly; some of what they said I could overhear.

'No. Which?' she asked.

'I don't care.'

'Wouldn't you want a boy?'

'I'd be happy whatever I got.'

'I know but which would you *rather* have? Don't men want boys?'

'I don't care. You.'

Somewhat later, Mohn's truck passed on the other side of the street. The milkman, well-bundled, sat behind headlights in a warm orange volume the size of a phone booth, steering one-handed and smoking a cigar that he set on the edge of the dashboard when, his wire carrier vibrant, he ran out of the truck with bottles. His passing led Neil to decide the time had come. Margaret woke up frightened of her father; we hissed our farewells and thanks to her quickly. Neil dropped the other girl off at her house a few blocks away; he knew where it was. Sometime during the night I must have seen this girl's face, but I have no memory of it. She is always behind a magazine or in the dark or with her back turned. Neil married her years later, I know, but after we arrived in Chicago I never saw him again either.

Red dawn light touched the clouds above the black slate roofs as, with a few other cars, we drove through Alton. The moon-sized clock of a beer billboard said ten after six. Olinger was deathly still. The air brightened as we moved along the highway; the glowing wall of my home hung above the woods as we rounded the long curve by the Mennonite dairy. With a .22 I could have hit a pane of my parents' bedroom window, and they were dreaming I was in Indiana. My grandfather would be up, stamping around in the kitchen for my grandmother to make him breakfast, or outside, walking to see if any ice had formed on the brook. For an instant I genuinely feared he might hail me from the peak of the barn roof. Then trees interceded and we were safe in a landscape where no one cared.

At the entrance to the Turnpike Neil did a strange thing, stopped the car and had me take the wheel. He had never trusted me to drive his father's car before; he had believed my not knowing where the crankshaft and fuel pump were handicapped my competence to steer. But now he was quite complacent. He hunched under an old mackinaw and leaned his head against the metal of the window frame and soon was asleep. We crossed the Susquehanna on a long smooth bridge below Harrisburg, then began climbing toward the Alleghenies. In the mountains there was snow, a dry dusting like sand, that waved back and forth on the road surface. Further along there had been a fresh fall that night, about two inches, and the plows had not yet cleared all the lanes. I was passing a Sunoco truck on a high curve when without warning the scraped section gave out and I realized I might skid into the fence if not over the edge. The radio was singing 'Carpets of clover, I'll lay right at your feet,' and the speedometer said 85. Nothing happened; the car stayed firm in the snow and Neil slept through the danger, his face turned skyward and his breath struggling in his nose. It was the first time I heard a contemporary of mine snore.

When we came into tunnel country the flicker and hollow amplification stirred Neil awake. He sat up, the mackinaw dropping to his lap, and lit a cigarette. A second after the scratch of his match occurred the moment of which each following moment was a slight diminution, as we made the long irregular descent toward Pittsburgh. There were many reasons for my feeling so happy. We were on our way. I had seen a dawn. This far, Neil could appreciate, I had brought us safely. Ahead, a girl waited who, if I asked, would marry me, but first there was a vast trip: many hours and towns interceded between me and that encounter. There was the quality of the 10 a.m. sunlight as it existed in the air ahead of the windshield, filtered by the thin overcast, blessing irresponsibility – you felt you could slice forever through such a cool pure element – and springing, by implying how high these hills had become, a wide-spreading pride: Pennsylvania, your state – as if you had made your life. And there was knowing that twice since midnight a person had trusted me enough to fall asleep beside me.

Activities

Miriam

Background notes

Truman Capote was born in New Orleans in 1924 and raised in Louisiana and Alabama. He received little formal education, and at the age of fifteen was working as a tap-dancer on a Mississippi riverboat. In New York he worked as an office boy on *The New Yorker* magazine and soon began publishing his own stories and novels, among these *Other Voices, Other Rooms*. Much of his work is concerned with the strange and macabre.

Pair work

1 Who or what is Miriam?
2 What sort of story is *Miriam*? Jot down together the different features of the story, e.g. elements of mystery, suspense, horror, etc. and decide together what type of story this is.

Group work

1 Look closely at the story and select together all the details about Miriam and Mrs Miller's feelings about her. Does the author make Miriam into a sinister presence or is it that Mrs Miller is gradually going mad?
2 Imagine that a television company is planning to make a short television play based on *Miriam*. They need some suggestions about how to get the atmosphere for the story, and have asked you to provide these in the form of storyboards.
Plan a storyboard for each scene and decide on the setting and special effects you would want to create the right atmosphere.

Written assignments

1 Try writing part of the camera script for a television adaptation of *Miriam*. You might produce a detailed script for one or two more scenes using your storyboards as the basis for this.
2 Write an analysis to show how the author has structured the story, so that it is uncertain whether this is a tale of the supernatural or of

nervous breakdown. Think about the narrative perspective and the use of the dream sequence and unreal details alongside details of everyday life.

3   Mystery or ghost stories tend to work through subtle suggestion rather than horrific descriptions. Try writing a piece of your own which avoids gruesome details but makes the ordinary seem mysterious and sinister.

Thank You, M'am

Background notes

Langston Hughes, born in 1902 in Joplin, Missouri, and raised in Kansas, is generally regarded as one of the most important black American writers. He thought of himself as primarily a poet – and was strongly influenced in this by the jazz and blues music of the period. However, it is perhaps for his stories that he is best remembered. All his work expresses a profound concern with the experience of black Americans. He died in 1967.

Pair work

1   Should Mrs Jones simply have taken Roger to the police station and left the police to decide what to do with him?

2   Later he has several chances to run away but chooses to stay with Mrs Jones. What makes him stay on each occasion?

3   Produce a chart mapping out the events of the story. Show in your chart the points at which events could have taken a very different turn, e.g. Mrs Jones could have handed Roger over to the police.

4   Imagine that a police officer calls on Mrs Jones. Roger has been identified by a witness as a boy seen snatching bags and the police are trying to find out about him. Roger has mentioned Mrs Jones as a friend. The police officer has come to interview Mrs Jones about Roger's character. Improvise the interview in role.

Group work

1   What are Mrs Jones' motives in taking the boy to her home? Examine the description of her room and the meal she offers Roger. How might these have influenced him? Mrs Jones tells Roger that she has done wrong in her own life too. Should adults admit things like this to children? Decide together on what you think of Mrs Jones' treatment of Roger.

2   Are there any details in the story that help to explain why the boy tried to snatch the bag? What do the blue suede shoes symbolize for Roger?

Written assignments

1   Does the story turn out as you expected? Write a careful study of the story showing how the author keeps the reader wondering how matters will turn out. Use your chart showing alternative paths the plot might have taken to help you in this.
2   Some might say that Roger got off too lightly, others that this was the best way to show him that he was on the verge of becoming a criminal. Consider the whole story, commenting on the characters and the action and putting forward your interpretation of Mrs Jones' kind of justice.

Breakfast

Background notes

John Steinbeck was born in 1902 in Salinas, California. After studying biology at Stanford University, he turned to journalism and then fiction. He was deeply affected by the Depression of the 1930s, and much of his best fiction is concerned with the hardships faced by impoverished farming communities. Several of his novels have been made into successful films. These include *Grapes of Wrath*, *East of Eden* and *Of Mice and Men*. He was awarded the Nobel Prize for Literature in 1962 and died in 1968.

Pair work

1   The narrator stresses how the memory of that breakfast gives him a 'curious, warm pleasure'; why do you think this memory is so special?
2   Look together for details in the description that reflect the warmth of this memory for the narrator.

Group work

1   Is this really a story or just a description? Come to a decision in your group.
2   If you consider it a story, what actually happens? If you feel it is more of a description, what is the writer trying to communicate through the description?

Written assignments

1   Rewrite the story, or part of it, from the young woman's point of view. Try to include some of the aspects of the character as she is portrayed by Steinbeck.
2   Imagine that this is just the beginning of a much longer story. Do not attempt to write this longer piece but write what script writers call a 'treatment', that is, a kind of plot summary covering all the important events and scenes to come.

Superman and Paula Brown's New Snowsuit

Background notes

Sylvia Plath was born in Boston in 1932. In America she studied at Smith College and in Britain at Cambridge Univeristy, where she met and married the poet, Ted Hughes. She is best known as a poet, though she wrote one novel, *The Bell Jar*, and several short stories. She committed suicide in 1963 at the age of thirty-one.

Pair work

1   Why does Uncle Frank say that they will pay for the snowsuit?
2   The story might have been called simply *Paula Brown's New Snowsuit*. What difference is made by the mention of Superman?

Group work

1   Uncle Frank says, 'ten years from now no one will ever know the difference'. The narrator says at the beginning of the story 'even now, thirteen years later'; why do you think she remembers what happened so vividly?
2   Improvise the conversation between the group of children the next time they meet to play in the street. Each take on a role of one of the characters with one group member acting as an observer of the conversation. When the role play is over, the observer should report back to the group on their performances and the conclusions drawn.
3   How is the approach of war an important part of the story? How do the events of the story mirror events occurring in Europe during the 1930s?

Written assignments

1 Write a commentary exploring the narrator's character and feelings during and after the snowsuit incident. Consider what the author is trying to show us about growing up. Include your view of the other characters in the story and their actions.

2 Change the format of the story into a diary and record the narrator's thoughts during the days leading up to the snowsuit incident and immediately afterwards.

Sweat

Background notes

Zora Neale Hurston was born in 1902 (or perhaps 1903) in Eatonville, Florida. Despite being beaten both at school and at home to 'break her spirit', she remained a spirited and confident girl. Later she studied anthropology at college and it was while she was researching the folklore of the Deep South that she began writing fiction. Her stories, which often blend autobiography and elements of folklore, express her own independence of spirit and a deep pride in black people. She died in poverty in 1960.

Pair work

1 Work individually for a moment and jot down whether you think Delia should be considered a murderer. Discuss together your views and prepare a short statement for the class expressing your joint view.

2 How do you feel about Bertha, the other woman? Is she at least partially responsible for what happens?

3 Imagine that the two women meet by accident soon after Jones' death. Either improvise their conversation or discuss what you think they would say to each other.

Group work

1 What has happened to the marriage between Delia and Sykes Jones? Work together and jot down how we learn about this through the story. It might be useful to divide the relationship into stages, for example, premarriage, early marriage and then the later years. Prepare a chart of the relationship to present to the rest of the class.

2 Is Delia a heroine? Is this a story about her triumph? Discuss her character and the way she is presented to us. Should we view her as a good woman?

3   Reread the section of the story where the group of men discuss Delia and Jones; one even suggests that they ought to kill Jones. What does their discussion reveal about the relationships between men and women in the society portrayed? You will need to work through the section, reading closely and relating their comments to the rest of the conversations and events.

Written assignments

1   Take any section of the story and rewrite it from Sykes' point of view. What view does he have of his own life and conduct? What makes him treat Delia the way he does? Try to answer some of these questions through your portrayal of Jones.

2   Write a scene from after the end of the story in which the men meet again and discuss what has happened to Jones. You need to decide first what they would actually know of Jones' death and how much they might guess.

3   Write two accounts of the funeral of Jones: one which might have appeared in the local paper and one which is an account by one of the characters who was present.

The Conversion of the Jews

Background notes

Philip Roth was born in 1933 in Newark, New Jersey, into a middle-class Jewish family. After university and a brief spell in the army, he became an English teacher. Roth has written both novels and short stories, including *Portnoy's Complaint* and *The Ghost Writer*. Roth's work, which often brings together autobiography and fantasy, is essentially comic though written with what he describes as 'serious playfulness'.

Pair work

1   Do you think Ozzie is justified in going up on to the roof? Are any of the other characters in some way responsible for what he does?

2   Consider the title. How do you interpret it?

3   Ozzie falls into the firemen's net. It looks like 'an overgrown halo'.

Why do you think the story ends with this reference to a religious sign? What effect does this have?

Group work

1 You may or may not know much about religion, but using your general knowledge and your opinions discuss together what the story tries to show about religion. Decide at some point in your discussion whether you would call this a religious story.

2 Think about the humorous tone of the story. Look at key moments where the author uses humour and his naïve central character, Ozzie, to help make a serious point.

3 Ozzie has had his moment of triumph but what will happen now? Work out together what you think will happen that night and on the following day and share these ideas as part of a class discussion.

Written assignments

1 Ozzie's escapade is quite spectacular. Write a newspaper account for the front page of the local paper; you might include some quotes from various people who were at the scene.

2 Draw on the work you have done on what might happen to Ozzie next to write his diary entry for the night of his adventure. You could then write a comparative diary entry for Rabbi Binder.

3 *The Conversion of the Jews* manages to look at the importance of religion but in a humorous way. What is your view about the importance of religion in your society? This is a complex question and you may well need to talk through your ideas with others before attempting to express them in writing.

Dry September

Background notes

William Faulkner, acknowledged as one of America's greatest writers, was born in 1897. He grew up in the South in Oxford, Mississippi, where he lived for most of his life. It is in this area that he sets his fictional Yoknapatawpha County. In a series of novels and short stories he chronicles the history of its families and colourful individuals from the American Civil War to the mid-twentieth century. Some of Faulkner's fiction is experimental, for example *Intruder in the Dust*, which makes it quite challenging. In 1950 he was awarded the Nobel Prize for Literature. He died in 1962.

Pair work

1 Who would you blame for the death of Will Hayes? Is there one person you consider to be the chief culprit or are there several? Work out together who you blame and prepare a statement on your decisions to compare with that of another pair.

2 Why does the story finish with McLendon? What effect does the author create by ending it at McLendon's house? Read the final section together very carefully and prepare your comments for class discussion.

Group work

1 What did happen to Minnie Cooper? What do we learn about her that explains what happened to Will Hayes? Prepare an explanation for the class on what part Minnie Cooper plays in Will Hayes' death.

2 Do you find the events of the story believable? Did such things really happen, do they still happen? Pool all your knowledge about the history of the Southern States of America and also what you have learned from the story to justify your answer.

3 What do you think will happen to Hawk, the barber, as a result of his actions? Either discuss together what you think will happen to him or improvise a scene at the barber's shop that takes place the following Monday.

Written assignments

1 Choose one of the other characters and rewrite the ending of the story focusing on his or her final actions. Write a commentary afterwards about why you chose that character and what you wanted to show through your alternative ending.

2 What will be the impact on the local community of Will Hayes' death and Minnie Cooper's breakdown at the picture show? You could write a continuation of the story which involves most of the characters we have met, showing their reactions. Or you might imitate the style of the story and write a description of the town and people which visits each main character to show how they are feeling.

3 Write a study of the story explaining your own reactions to it and considering some of its features. You might want to refer to its setting and choice of vocabulary and the structure of the story: especially the way it moves from one character's point of view to another's. You may also want to look at the story as an exploration of a Southern community's prejudices about black people and white women, etc. You could select just one or two of these aspects to discuss in depth.

Misty, Tiled Chambers

Background notes

Valerie Miner was born in New York and grew up in New Jersey, the Pacific Northwest and California. She has travelled widely, and has worked both as a journalist and as a teacher. Strongly committed to the international women's movement, she writes fiction which explores the challenges faced by contemporary women.

Pair work

1   Gerry learns how to swim by the end of the story but what else is different about her?
2   Make a list of any changes that you agree on, noting down which parts of the story provide you with evidence.
3   Are Gerry's initial feelings about Mitch understandable? How would you have reacted in a similar situation?

Group work

1   Locate what you consider to be the main scenes in the story and make a chart showing these. The story has many very precise descriptions which help us to visualize it. Imagine that the story is to appear in a new collection of stories, and that it will have two illustrations.
2   Using your chart, choose together the moments that should be illustrated and be prepared to explain your choices to the class.
3   What makes Gerry's mom so keen on the swimming, even when the nuns are displeased about it? Was it fair to make Gerry learn how to swim?
4   Imagine that Gerry and her mother are summoned once more to the school to discuss their reasons for Gerry taking swimming lessons. Set up a role play in which some of you play the nuns and others play Gerry and her mother. What conclusions do you come to?

Written assignments

1   Gerry is in trouble with the nuns for the essay about her swimming lessons. Write her essay or a part of it and then add your own commentary about what you tried to show about her character through your writing.

2 Write a review of this story commenting on the main themes and characters, the way it is written, and explaining whether you would recommend it to someone of your own age. Try reading a book review section in a monthly or weekly magazine first. Think about the style of these reviews as you plan and write your own.

The Catbird Seat

Background notes

James Thurber is perhaps America's best-known humorist of the Twentieth century. After studying at Ohio State Univesity he worked as a journalist, beginning his long association with *The New Yorker* magazine in the late 1920s. He wrote stories, essays, fables and sketches, many of them illustrated with his own distinctive drawings. His work is characterized by domineering women and sad, rather timid men who dream of escape from their current lives. Thurber died in 1961.

Pair work

1 Which of the main characters do you sympathize with, Mr Martin or Mrs Barrows? Are either sympathetic?
2 At what point in the story did you feel that Mr Martin would not 'rub out' Mrs Barrows?
3 Imagine that Mrs Barrows and Mr Martin meet by accident a few months after the end of the story. Decide on how they would feel at the sight of each other, then improvise their thoughts and conversation during their meeting.

Group work

1 What do you consider the title to mean? Prepare your view for explaining to the class and decide on an alternative title of your own.
2 The story contains a number of phrases popular in baseball. Track them down in a reference book and make a note of their meanings.
3 Do all sports have phrases like this? Choose one sport that your group is familiar with and list any phrases that have special meaning in the sport.
4 A misogynist is a woman hater. Is the author of this story a misogynist?

Written assignments

1 Mrs Barrows will now need a new job, perhaps Mr Martin may be promoted. Write a reference for each of them. You can invent some details but try to make use of all the evidence you can from the story.

2 Imagine that Mrs Barrows sues Fitweiler for wrongful dismissal and that a hearing is held at which Mr Martin is called to answer questions. Write a script of part or all of the scene.

3 Select a section from the story and rewrite it from either Mrs Barrows' or Fitweiler's point of view.

A New England Nun

Background notes

Mary E. Wilkins Freeman was born in 1852 in Randolph, Massachusetts. Her early life was one of genteel poverty, and this story reflects this. Her stories are set in the small farming communities of Massachusetts and her characters are often humble, ordinary people struggling to retain their individuality in the face of daily hardships. Her writing is tempered by a wry humour.

Pair work

1 Given what you know of her life and character, do you think Louisa makes the right decision?

2 Does the narrator want us to admire and approve of Louisa or show us that she is strange in some way? Pick out some details from the story to support your point of view.

3 Imagine that Joe Dagget dies quite suddenly and that Louisa and Joe's widow, Lily, meet in Louisa's home to talk over what they now feel. Improvise their conversation.

Group work

1 Is this a story without a villain? Make notes on each character and decide whether you feel anyone is responsible for what happens.

2 The style of the story changes from the highly descriptive and reflective in the main part of the story to the active and dialogue-based style of the later scene between Joe and Lily. How does the structure of the story and this change of style enforce the differences in the main characters?

Written assignments

1 Imagine that Louisa and Joe meet a few years later. Write a short monologue by each of them as they each reflect on their meeting and their former feelings for each other. Use what you know of their characters to make the voices of the monologues those of Louisa and Joe.

2 Write about a room at home or at school that you are very familiar with using a similar highly detailed style to the one in the story. Louisa's house is calm and serene, but it may be that the details of your room create a very different atmosphere.

The Ambitious Guest

Background notes

Nathaniel Hawthorne, born in 1804, is one of America's first great writers. He came from a distinguished family in Salem, Massachusetts, and was keenly aware of his Puritan ancestry. Much of his best fiction is set in the New England colonies of the Seventeenth century. His stories often explore the darker aspects of life. He died in 1864.

Pair work

1 What kind of story is this? Between you, agree on one word to describe the story, e.g. horror, tragedy, disaster, moral etc. and be ready to explain to the class why you chose that particular word.

2 Look at the description of the landscape around the cottage. What effect is created by this and what is the relationship between human actions and nature around them?

3 What can you tell about the age of the story from the language used in it? Make a list of any key words or phrases that you feel are evidence of your ideas about the story's age.

Group work

1 In your group, make a chart showing the events in the story that lead up to the 'Slide'.

2 Agree on what you feel is the main point or moral of the story. How does this relate to its title?

3   Compare the chart of events that you prepared with your view of the story's point. Discuss how the author has built up his meaning during the course of the story.

4   What is your answer to the question at the end of the story? Why does Hawthorne leave a question at the end?

Written assignments

1   Write an eyewitness account of the scene by the next traveller passing through the Notch. They see the devastation caused by the 'Slide' and enter the house to see who has survived.

2   Write a newspaper report of the disaster for the local paper. Think carefully about the date of the story and the nature of the tragedy. You could decide to give your article a particular slant, e.g. the human tragedy angle or solving the mystery of the visitor to the cottage.

The Idea in the Back of My Brother's Head

Background notes

William Saroyan was born in 1908 into an Armenian community in rural California. It is this colourful, close-knit community of larger-than-life characters which he depicts with warmth and humour in his best work. He wrote a great deal (essays, plays, stories, novels, reminiscences) using what he described as a loose 'jump-in-the-river-and-start-to-swim' style. He died in 1981.

Pair work

1   Would you go on a five-day journey with old Henry? Imagine that you are a friend of the narrator's. Role play the scene in which you give him advice about going on the trip. Take it in turns with your partner to play the roles of friend and narrator and then discuss the different advice to come out of the role play.

2   In a good short story every character adds a little to the overall meaning of the story. What do you think each character adds to our understanding here? Make a list of the characters and note down significant details about them using evidence from the story. Use your notes as starting points for a class discussion.

Group work

1 We keep hearing the peacock in the story. Work together and decide what you think makes the author draw the reader's attention to the sound and appearance of the bird at several points in the plot. What associations does the peacock image have for you? How do these compare with the way this author has used the image?

2 There are no individual female characters in the story, only 'the women'. Discuss together what you feel the author's intentions are in presenting them in this way.

Written assignments

1 Describe the scene when old Henry and the narrator arrive back after their five-day journey. Try to match something of the style of the original story in your description.

2 What kind of character is old Henry? The narrator gives us his own view but we also learn more about Henry than the narrator actually knows, for example from Uncle Gotto. Write a study of old Henry's character.

3 Many people associate America with the idea of travel because it is so huge and so varied a country. Try writing a piece about an American journey. This could be about an imaginary trip to somewhere you have always wanted to visit or about a real trip that you have undertaken.

The Happiest I've Been

Background notes

John Updike was born in Shillington, Pennsylvania, in 1932. On graduating from Harvard he spent a year in Britain at Oxford University studying art. He became a full-time writer after working as a journalist on *The New Yorker*. His main subject is everyday middle-class America, which he depicts with what has been called 'a critical though compassionate realism'. He is perhaps at his best when writing about adolescence as he does in this story.

Pair work

1 Look carefully over the story together and identify what makes Neil and the narrator close friends. Does the nature of their friendship change during the story? If so, how?

2   Make a list of the key points about their characters, noting similarities and differences.

Group work

1   What makes the narrator so happy at the end of the story? How does he feel he has 'moved on' since leaving his home the night before?

2   The story is clearly American because of the language and the setting but is the story about America or could its events have taken place in this country?

3   Work on a section together and try to 'translate' it, i.e. to change spellings, words and phrases into Standard English. It would be useful for later class discussion if each group chooses a different part of the story to work on. Decide also where in your country would be an equivalent kind of town to Olinger and the other places which are mentioned. Add these to your 'translation'.

Written assignments

1   Look again at the party scenes in the story and produce Neil's account of these events.

2   The story itself contains very little action, but a lot of reflection on the part of the narrator. Write a commentary on the story explaining the issues it is concerned with and how effectively it conveys these to the reader.

3   The narrator explains that the most important thing about his friendship with Neil is that they have both lived with their grandparents. You may or may not have grandparents of your own, but you will probably have views about how different generations may influence each other. Write a story or essay considering the particular kind of relationship that may exist between grandparent and grandchild (or between a child and an older friend or relative).

Extended Activities

1 What picture of America do you gain from these stories? How does it compare with what you know about America from other sources like television and film?

2 Prejudice is often a theme in American literature and there are a number of stories that deal with this issue in the collection. Write about the stories that you felt dealt with prejudice in a powerful way.

3 What do you think of the way women are portrayed in the collection? Do you gain any sense of the role women have played in American life from the stories?

4 Many of the stories contain humour. Pick out the stories that seem funniest to you explaining why they appeal. Does the humour help to convey a more serious message in the chosen stories?

5 If you were to recommend just one story from the collection for a friend to read, which one would it be and why would you choose it?

6 What have you noticed about American English compared to British English? Using evidence from the stories show how the two versions of English are different.

7 Comparing and contrasting two stories can be a way of gaining a better understanding of both. The following list provides some suggested pairs that you might write about but you can of course think of your own:– *Sweat* and *Dry September*; *Superman and Paula Brown's New Snowsuit* and *Misty, Tiled Chambers*; *A New England Nun* and *Miriam*; *The Conversion of the Jews* and *Misty, Tiled Chambers*.

8 The stories in this collection reflect the cultural diversity of the population of America. Choose two or more stories and show how the different cultures that they draw upon are reflected in the storylines, characters and the language employed by the authors, e.g. the Armenian background of William Saroyan and Black American background of Langston Hughes.

9 Imagine that a British film company wants to make three short television films for British viewers to help them understand some of the important issues in American life; they want to adapt existing stories. Recommend the three stories that seem to you best suited to this purpose bearing in mind both their qualities as stories and what would make them work well through the medium of television.

Wider Reading

Truman Capote

Other Voices, Other Rooms, Picador classics, 1988 (novel)
A Truman Capote Reader, Abacus Books, 1989

Langston Hughes

Big Sea, Paperback Serpent's Tail, 1987
The Selected Poems of Langston Hughes, Paperback Serpent's Tail, 1987

John Steinbeck

Of Mice and Men, Penguin Modern Classics, 1969 (novel)
The Grapes of Wrath, Mandarin, 1990 (novel)
East of Eden, Mandarin, 1990 (novel)

Sylvia Plath

The Bell Jar, Faber & Faber, 1967 (novel)
Johnny Panic and the Bible of Dreams, Faber & Faber, 1979 (stories)

Zora Neale Hurston

I Love Myself When I Am Laughing... A Zora Neale Hurston Reader, ed.
Alice Walker, The Feminist Press (N.Y.), 1985
Dust Tracks on a Road, Virago, 1988 (autobiography)

Philip Roth

Portnoy's Complaint, Penguin, 1986 (novel)
The Ghost Writer, Cape, 1979 (novel)
A Philip Roth Reader, Penguin, 1984

William Faulkner

The Sound and the Fury, Picador, 1989 (novel)
Intruder in the Dust, Picador, 1989 (novel)
The Collected Stories of William Faulkner, Penguin 20th Century
Classics, 1989

Valerie Miner

Blood Sisters, Paperback Women's Press, 1981 (novel)
Trespassing, Methuen, 1989 (stories)

James Thurber

Vintage Thurber, Penguin, 1983 (stories, sketches and essays)
Fables for Our Time and Famous Poems Illustrated, Mandarin, 1991
Middle-aged Man on the Flying Trapeze, Methuen, 1984

Mary E. Wilkins Freeman

A Humble Romance, 1987
A New England Nun and Other Stories, 1891
The Shoulders of Atlas, 1908

Nathaniel Hawthorne

Young Goodman Brown and Other Tales, Oxford, 1987 (stories)
The Scarlet Letter and Selected Tales, Penguin, 1983 (novel and stories)

William Saroyan

The Daring Young Man on the Flying Trapeze, Faber & Faber (stories)
The Whole Voyald, Faber & Faber (stories)

John Updike

Rabbit, Run, Penguin, 1969 (novel)
The Centaur, Penguin, 1970 (novel)
Pigeon Feathers, Penguin, (stories)

General Introduction to American Literature

An Outline of American Literature, Peter B. High, Longman, 1986